as seen on channel four

JAMIE OLIVER

jamie's dinners

the essential cookbook

I LOVE TANYA ROBINSON

JAMIE OLIVER

jamie's dinners

with photographs by david loftus and chris terry
and illustrations by marion deuchars

PENGUIN BOOKS

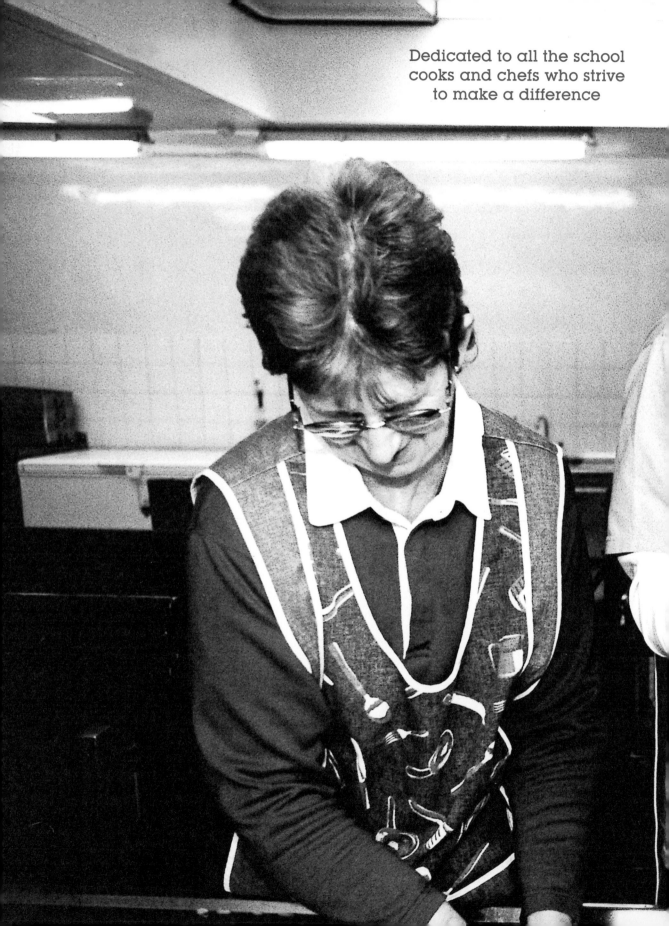

Dedicated to all the school cooks and chefs who strive to make a difference

PENGUIN BOOKS

UK | USA | Canada | Ireland | Australia
India | New Zealand | South Africa

Penguin Books is part of the Penguin Random House group of companies
whose addresses can be found at global.penguinrandomhouse.com

First published by Michael Joseph 2004
Published in Penguin Books 2006
Reissued in this edition 2019
001

A CIP catalogue record for this book is available from the British Library

ISBN: 978–0–718–18831–3

penguin.co.uk

jamieoliver.com

www.greenpenguin.co.uk

Penguin Random House is committed to a
sustainable future for our business, our readers
and our planet. This book is made from Forest
Stewardship Council® certified paper.

contents

Introduction viii

The Top Ten 1

Family Tree 30

Five-Minute Wonders 58

Sarnies 72

Salads 104

Soups 138

Vegetables 158

Pasta 180

Meat 212

Fish 248

Desserts 282

Kitchens That Work 308

Thanks 312

Index 314

INTRODUCTION

I'm really proud of this book because it's full of recipes for great family dinners, and what I want is to get you all cooking and enjoying them together at home. I've noticed, as I continue to work as a chef and grow as a parent, that there are a whole bunch of people who just don't cook at all, or do so very rarely. But I truly believe that anyone can cook and love it – and that everyone has it in them to hold great dinner parties, family occasions or everyday meals that are remembered for a long time. What I hope this book will do is show that anyone can have a go at cooking. It's totally aimed at families and at those who have an interest in good food, no matter what your budget is. Probably someone like you!

Over the last two and a half years I've been researching and filming a documentary series looking at the food being served in British schools, to see if we can cook tasty and nutritious meals for school kids. I decided to use the same idea in my approach to this book, which means the food is cheap, economical, accessible, easy and time-efficient to make. We all want the same things when making dinner at home for our families.

All the major factors that are needed to make a good affordable school dinner also apply to a mindful, clever cook at home. Availability, accessibility, regionality, affordability, simplicity and a tasty product are the key, with not too much washing-up if you're lucky! Just taking all these words has provided me with a great brief for this cookbook. It's not concerned with fillet steak and lobster and posh stuff. Most of the recipes use pretty standard ingredients that you can buy from street markets or supermarkets all over the country, if not the world.

I think you'll get a lot out of these chapters. They concern themselves with the types of food that most of us are eating every day. For instance, there is a lovely little chapter called Five-Minute Wonders, which gives you eight fantastically quick recipes. Perfect for busy lives as each one only takes five minutes or so. I hope a chapter like The Top Ten is really going to inspire you. It's like *Top of the Pops*, but for food, and it gives you ten crowd-pleasers that everyone loves to eat. The Family Tree chapter takes recipes like a simple tomato sauce or pesto and shows you how to take them further by changing and tweaking here and there, so you can make a whole handful of dishes from just one recipe. I've also included a chapter on sandwiches – you might think this sounds a bit naff, but it's great because it acknowledges that sandwiches are the most widely eaten food product in most western countries. I've tried to show you how you can make really good portable meals to make your work colleagues or friends jealous at lunchtime! Have a look at the picture of the lunchbox on page 76. Then all your normal chapters follow, like Pasta, Meat and Fish. With Vegetables I've kept things really chatty and shown you that veggies can be a real highlight to your dinner, not just an extra. I've given you various different ways of cooking each vegetable so you can widen your repertoire.

I was brought up around food, around chefs and cooks, and I also love nature, agriculture and farming, the changing seasons and the produce that comes with them. You may feel the same way as I do about these things – however, I do think a lot of people just don't understand the importance of where their food comes from or what might have been done to it before they buy it. It's good to question these things.

First, good-quality food and produce – and yes, this may involve organics – is always considered to be middle-class or rich people's food. Wrong. I've worked with students and people on the dole who eat better than some city boys earning hundreds of thousands of pounds a year, and the reason is that they use their heads when buying. Why is this important? Why should you have standards when buying? Because you're going to put this food in your mouth and swallow it and you'll do this two or three times every single day of your life. Everything you eat contributes to you being happy, or fit, or lethargic, or full of energy, or susceptible to colds and flu, or being able to think better and hold your concentration. Your hair, your fingernails, your height, your skin, everything you are is made from the food you eat.

my beautiful family

Very rarely does anyone go into a garage, phone shop or shoe shop and ask for 'the cheapest, most rubbish one'. So why do we walk into supermarkets and support those companies that are producing cheap products? As a general rule, when food is cheap the quality is not going to be so good. All supermarkets have got to push forward, try harder to support regional, or at least British, produce and strive for more integrity.

It all comes down to your perception of value – is it about buying the cheapest thing you can get, or is it about spending a little more and getting something that tastes nicer, smells better and makes you feel good in return? People in Britain spend the smallest percentage of their weekly wage on food compared to most of the rest of Europe. Europeans tend to spend more on better produce. I think it's a matter of priorities. For instance, before I got married, if I'd suggested that we go out to a half-decent restaurant to spend £25 to £30 on a meal, with a few bottles of wine to get tiddly, my friends would not have been interested in the slightest, but if I'd said, 'Why don't we go to the local nightclub?' where we'd have ended up spending £50 on drinks, even my friends who were unemployed or on the dole would have found the money somehow. I don't think it always comes down to money, I think it's a priority thing.

I'd never try to persuade you to unnecessarily spend more money, but I'd really like you to spend the money you've got more wisely when shopping for food. I've got friends who are unemployed and have time on their hands, yet they fill their shopping trolleys with packets of processed food and soft drinks, with no veggies in sight. And yet this is the most expensive way to feed your family. It is much cheaper to buy fresh produce and cook it than to heat up pre-packaged, processed food. There really isn't much excuse for not giving cooking a go.

Whether I'm at home with my family, or at work with my surrogate family at the restaurant, I enjoy sitting down to eat and chat with them. So what I hope will happen with this book is that you'll get stuck in and enjoy some of these recipes with your friends and family.

my surrogate family
at fifteen

THE TOP TEN

SAUSAGE + MASH & ONION GRAVY

JACKET POTATO

WITH PRAWNS & MARIE ROSE SAUCE

MY FAVOURITE TOO

APPLE PIE

TOMATO SOUP

CHICKEN TIKKA MASALA

CHICKEN & LEEK PIE

MY FAVOURITES

FISH & CHIPS

As this is a friendly book about everyday dinners for all of us, I thought I'd hit you with a collection of favourite dishes early on and not muck about! But I don't just want to give you my own thoughts (although, if you're interested, I've listed my personal favourites below!). We're always hearing about Top Tens for music, films and books, so, knowing that every one of you will have your own Top Ten dinners, I asked people who visit my website to write in and tell me about their favourite food. Over the course of about six months I had thousands of ideas coming in from all over the world and, although they differed from country to country, it was interesting to see that we all have favourites in common. So this chapter is based on ten dishes that I love to cook and eat with my family, but that are also your favourites.

MY FAVOURITE DINNERS...

Mum's superb roasted chicken; spaghetti arrabiatta; a spicy noodle laksa soup; a fantastic bacon sandwich; the ultimate steak and chips; simply poached salmon with asparagus, new potatoes and homemade mayonnaise; Peking roasted duck and pancakes; shepherd's pie; fish pie; fruit pie (apple or cherry); rhubarb crumble...

... and now we're over ten, you see! And that's without even mentioning roast leg of lamb, spaghetti bolognese or meatballs, all of which I love... It's very hard to narrow it down to ten!

THE BEST SAUSAGE & SUPER MASH WITH ONION GRAVY

I really love this recipe for sausage and mash – you must have a go at it! I made it on Bonfire Night last year, inspired by my mate Peter Gott's award-winning Cumberland sausages. If you can't get hold of the traditional curled sausage, just roll up a string of about six normal ones to give you a similar shape. You will need some wooden skewers or long, sharpened rosemary sticks.

SERVES 4

2 long, curled Cumberland
  sausages or 6 regular sausages
2 cloves of garlic, peeled and
  finely sliced
1 bunch of fresh sage, leaves picked
olive oil
1 bunch of fresh rosemary, leaves
  picked
2kg potatoes, peeled

300ml milk
80g unsalted butter
4 tablespoons freshly grated
  horseradish, or use jarred
4 medium red onions, peeled
  and finely sliced
5 tablespoons balsamic or red
  wine vinegar
1 quality beef or chicken stock cube

Preheat the oven to 200°C/400°F/gas 6. If you're using the traditional round Cumberland sausage, tuck the garlic and most of the sage leaves between the layers of sausage. If you're using normal sausages, untwist the links and squeeze the meat through, rolling them into a tight circle and pushing in the garlic and sage as you go. Secure the sausages with a couple of skewers or some sharp rosemary stalks. Place on an oiled baking tray, drizzle with oil and sprinkle them with the rosemary leaves. Roast in the oven for 20 minutes, or until golden and crisp. Around 5 minutes before the sausages are ready, remove the tray from the oven, place the rest of the sage leaves next to the sausages, drizzle with oil, then return to the oven – the leaves will go lovely and crisp.

While the sausages are cooking, chop the potatoes into rough chunks and cook in boiling salted water until tender. Drain well, then mash until smooth, adding the milk, 70g of the butter and the horseradish (use more if needed). Season to taste with sea salt and black pepper, then put the lid on the pan and keep warm until needed.

Making the onion gravy is simple. Fry the onions – really slowly – in a little oil, covered, for about 15 minutes, or until soft. Remove the lid, turn the heat up, and as soon as the onions become golden, pour in the vinegar and boil until it almost disappears. Turn the heat down again, add the rest of the butter, crumble in the stock cube and 550ml of water and stir well. Simmer to a nice gravy consistency. To serve, dollop some oozy potatoes on the plate, chop up the sausages (discarding the skewers), put them alongside the mash, and spoon over the onion gravy. Scatter with the crispy sage leaves. Proper comfort food!

CALORIES	FAT	SAT FAT	PROTEIN	CARBS	SUGAR	SALT	FIBRE
897kcal	39.2g	18.3g	29g	113.8g	24.6g	2.6g	12.9g

THE ULTIMATE BURGER & CHIPS

One of the best meals in the world is burger and chips, and this burger is fantastic. Buy some good chuck steak, then either pulse it in a food processor or ask your butcher to mince it up for you – that way you always know what's in it. And the chips are so fantastic, far healthier than the deep-fried variety. The rosemary salt can be kept for months in a little airtight jar and has a fantastic, intense flavour that is great with chicken or pork chops, too.

SERVES 8

1kg chuck steak or quality
    minced steak
1 onion, peeled and finely chopped
olive oil
1 pinch of cumin seeds
1 tablespoon coriander seeds
1 handful of freshly grated
    Parmesan cheese
1 heaped tablespoon
    English mustard
1 large egg

100g breadcrumbs
8 burger buns

CHIPS
2kg large potatoes, skins left on, cut
    into 1cm-thick chips
olive oil
1 bulb of garlic
3 sprigs of fresh rosemary, leaves picked
1 lemon
85g sea salt

If you're using chuck steak to make the burgers, slice it up and pulse it in a food processor. Transfer the meat to a bowl. Slowly cook the onion in a large frying pan with a little oil for 5 minutes, or until softened. Add the onion to the meat – it will give sweetness to the burger. Using a pestle and mortar, bash up the cumin and coriander seeds with a pinch of sea salt and black pepper until fine and add to the meat. Add the Parmesan, mustard, egg and half the breadcrumbs and mix well. If the mixture is too sticky, add a few more breadcrumbs.

Lay some greaseproof paper on a tray and sprinkle over some of the remaining breadcrumbs. Shape the meat into 8 fat burgers and place these on top of the crumbs on the tray. Sprinkle more crumbs on top and press down gently. Chill for 1 hour before cooking to firm up.

Half an hour before you want to cook the burgers, put a large flat baking tray in the oven and turn the heat to 230°C/450°F/gas 8. Parboil the chips for 10 minutes in boiling salted water, then drain. Heat some oil in a frying pan, smash the garlic bulb up and chuck in the cloves, then add the chips. Toss in the oil and season with black pepper, then transfer to the preheated tray and roast for 20 to 25 minutes, or until golden and crisp. Now make the rosemary salt. Bash the rosemary in a pestle and mortar, grate in the lemon zest and add the salt, then bash to a paste. Push this paste through a sieve and keep to one side until you're ready to serve.

CALORIES	FAT	SAT FAT	PROTEIN	CARBS	SUGAR	SALT	FIBRE
660kcal	18.2g	6.9g	40.2g	86.5g	7g	2g	6.5g

Take the burgers out of the fridge and fry them in a little oil on a medium-high heat for 8 to 10 minutes, depending on the thickness of the burgers and how you like them, turning occasionally. Serve on toasted burger buns, with tomato ketchup, and your fat chips sprinkled with pinches of rosemary salt. Other great things to top the burger with are layers of sliced beef tomatoes, thinly sliced cheese, raw onion rings, lettuce, a grating of fresh horseradish – even a fried egg!

SIMPLE BAKED LASAGNE

Lasagne is always best when made with fresh sheets of pasta, and these are now available in packets in all good supermarkets. Dried lasagne is fine as well, but it will need to be simmered gently to soften it before using. I haven't used a béchamel sauce because it takes too long – I've used a crème fraîche mixture that does a great job. A mixture of beef and pork is really tasty – it's just a brilliant sauce which can also be used for making spaghetti bolognese, stuffing cannelloni, mixing with sautéed mushrooms and pappardelle.

SERVES 10

4 slices of pancetta or smoked streaky
    bacon, finely sliced
1 pinch of cinnamon
1 onion, peeled and finely chopped
1 carrot, finely chopped
2 cloves of garlic, peeled and
    finely chopped
1 big bunch of fresh herbs, such as
    sage, oregano, rosemary, thyme
olive oil
400g shin of beef or stewing beef,
    minced coarsely
200g pork belly, skin off, minced
2 x 400g tins of quality plum tomatoes

2 glasses of red wine
2 fresh bay leaves
1 butternut squash, deseeded and
    roughly chopped
1 tablespoon coriander seeds, bashed
1 dried red chilli, bashed
400g fresh lasagne sheets
400g mozzarella cheese, torn up

WHITE SAUCE
500ml crème fraîche
3 anchovy fillets, in oil, finely chopped
2 handfuls of freshly grated
    Parmesan cheese
optional: a little milk

Preheat the oven to 180°C/350°F/gas 4. In a large casserole pan, slowly fry the pancetta and cinnamon until golden, then add the onion, carrot, garlic, herbs and 4 tablespoons of oil. Mix together, then add the beef and pork. Cook for 5 minutes, then add the tomatoes and the wine (or use water). Add the bay and bring to the boil. Wet a scrunched up piece of greaseproof paper and place on top of the pan and cover with a lid. Place in the oven for 2 hours or simmer on the hob over a gentle heat for 1 hour 30 minutes. Rub the squash with oil and sprinkle with sea salt, black pepper and the bashed-up coriander seeds and chilli. Place on a baking tray and roast in the oven for the last 45 minutes of cooking the sauce. When the sauce is done, season to taste and put aside. Mix the crème fraîche, anchovies, and a handful of Parmesan together, and season. Loosen the mixture with a little milk, if needed.

Turn the oven to 200°C/400°F/gas 6. To assemble, rub a lasagne dish with oil, lay lasagne sheets over the bottom and drape them over the sides (see pages 10 to 11). Add a layer of meat, a little white sauce and a sprinkling of Parmesan. Break the squash into pieces and use this as one layer, then repeat the layers, finishing with a layer of pasta covered in white sauce. Tear over the mozzarella and sprinkle with extra Parmesan. Cook in the oven for 30 to 35 minutes, or until golden.

CALORIES	FAT	SAT FAT	PROTEIN	CARBS	SUGAR	SALT	FIBRE
563kcal	27.5g	14.5g	31.9g	44.4g	10.9g	1.5g	3.8g

THE FAMOUS JACKET POTATO

There is nothing better when you're hungry than a hot, steaming, fluffy jacket potato. Even simply served with a knob of unsalted butter, or a drizzle of olive oil, or maybe a dollop of soured cream, and some sea salt and black pepper, it is one of the most comforting things to eat. The trouble is, most people think of jacket potatoes as nothing more than boring old high-street or canteen food, but they can actually be the basis of a really memorable, luxurious dinner. It just depends how you think about it. But the beauty of them is that they can be topped with some amazing combinations. I've decided to give you my favourite ways, including a recipe for making mini jackets by roasting some new potatoes in oil, garlic and rosemary – yum! – and one for sweet potatoes, which I think you will love.

To bake the potatoes, simply wash them, prick them with a fork so they don't explode in the oven, rub them with olive oil and sea salt, then place in the oven at 190°C/375°F/gas 5 for between 1 hour and 1 hour 20 minutes. The cooking time will depend on how large your spuds are. Split open the potatoes and add a small knob of unsalted butter to the centre of each before adding your chosen topping.

THREE CHEESES WITH CHIVES

Grate over some lovely Red Leicester followed by some Cheddar. Crumble up a little Roquefort or other blue cheese and sprinkle over the top. The heat from the potato will melt the cheeses together into a lovely oozy topping. Sprinkle over some finely chopped chives.

CRAB, CRÈME FRAÎCHE, SPRING ONIONS, CHILLI & MINT

For 4 people you will need 6 tablespoons of lovely freshly picked white crabmeat. Dress this with the juice of 1 lemon, twice as much extra virgin olive oil, sea salt and black pepper, 4 finely chopped spring onions, 1 small handful of finely chopped fresh mint and 1 fresh red chilli, deseeded and finely chopped. Add 1 tablespoon of crème fraîche to the crab mixture and divide between the 4 potatoes.

PRAWNS & MARIE ROSE SAUCE

For 4 people you will need 4 handfuls of prawns. To make the Marie Rose sauce, get 2 heaped tablespoons of mayonnaise, 1 tablespoon of ketchup, 1 teaspoon of brandy to give it a nice buzz and 1 pinch of cayenne pepper. Season with sea salt and black pepper and mix it all together. Squeeze over the juice from 1 lemon – enough to give it a twang – then dress the prawns with the Marie Rose sauce and spoon over the 4 potatoes. Sprinkle with cress and a little fresh parsley.

SMOKED SALMON & SOURED CREAM

When you split the potatoes open, make quite a large well in the centre and add a small knob of unsalted butter. Take 2 handfuls of the small inner leaves of a cos lettuce and mix with 1 handful of roughly chopped fresh flat-leaf parsley. Dress the leaves with 1 tablespoon of soured cream, 2 tablespoons of extra virgin olive oil and the juice of 1 lemon. Finish with a pinch of sea salt and black pepper and mix together well. Divide into 4 portions, then get 1 or 2 nice slices of smoked salmon and wrap them round a portion before lifting it carefully on to one of the waiting potatoes. Repeat with the other 3 portions. Serve with lemon wedges and extra black pepper. Lovely.

MINI JACKETS TOPPED WITH BEETROOT, COTTAGE CHEESE & HORSERADISH

If you don't fancy a big jacket potato, then try baking some new potatoes instead – lovely as a veg dish to go with meat or fish and perfect for a barbecue. For 4 people you'll need about 800g. Wash and prick them, then roll in some sea salt, olive oil and rosemary leaves and add them to a roasting tray. Take a whole bulb of garlic and break it up into cloves then scatter these, unpeeled, all over the potatoes. Place in the oven to roast for 45 to 50 minutes, or until soft in the middle and crispy outside. When the potatoes are cooked, serve topped with a little cottage cheese or soured cream and some diced vinegary beetroot. You can also grate over some fresh horseradish to give them a kick if you like. Sprinkle over some chopped fresh herbs, such as basil, parsley or chervil. These make great little canapés to munch before dinner!

SWEET POTATO TOPPED WITH CHILLIES, BUFFALO MOZZARELLA & BASIL

Sweet potatoes are lovely roasted, as the juices caramelize slightly where you prick the skin. They won't look much from the outside, but when you split them open the flesh will be a vibrant orange and so tasty. I love to top them with some torn-up pieces of buffalo mozzarella, some finely chopped fresh red and green chillies, a little squeeze of lemon juice and some fresh whole basil leaves, a drizzle of extra virgin olive oil and some sea salt and black pepper. You'll love it!

APPLE PIE

Obviously apple pie is one of the all-time classic desserts. I can't even imagine how good they must have tasted in the old days when England used to have hundreds and hundreds of different varieties of apples – they would have tasted like heaven. My tip to you is to use both cooking and eating apples in the filling. The best apple pies I've ever made are from apples bought at farmers' markets. As the year progresses it's also a treat to substitute some of the apples with beautiful pears, then wonderful blackberries.

SERVES 6

PASTRY
225g plain flour, plus
   extra for dusting
140g unsalted butter, plus
   extra for greasing
85g caster sugar
1 lemon
2 large egg yolks

FILLING
1 large Bramley cooking apple
4 eating apples (try Cox's or Braeburn)
3 tablespoons Demerara or
   muscovado sugar
½ a lemon
½ teaspoon ground ginger
1 handful of raisins or sultanas
1 large egg yolk mixed with
   a splash of milk

Preheat the oven to 180°C/350°F/gas 4. To make the pastry, put the flour, butter and caster sugar in a food processor, finely grate in the lemon zest, add a pinch of sea salt and pulse together. Add the egg yolks and a tiny drop of water and pulse again to a dough. Butter a 20cm metal pie dish – the reason for using a metal one is because it will conduct heat better so the bottom of the pie will cook at the same time as the top.

Divide the pastry in two and roll half of it out on a clean flour-dusted surface until ½cm thick. Lay the pastry in the metal dish and gently push it down into the sides. Don't worry if it tears or breaks – just patch it up and it will look nice and rustic! Pop the pie dish and the remaining pastry into the fridge while you peel the apples. Quarter the Bramley apple and cut the eating apples into eighths. Toss them in a small pan with the sugar, finely grate in the lemon zest, add the ginger, sultanas or raisins, and 1 tablespoon of water. Simmer gently for 5 minutes, or until the apples are just tender. Remove from the heat and allow to cool completely.

Remove the pie dish and pastry from the fridge and pack the apple mix tightly into the pie dish. Eggwash the pastry rim, then roll out the other half of the dough. Drape this over the top of the pie and roughly pinch the edges together using your finger and thumb and trim away any excess pastry. Eggwash the top, make a couple of small incisions and bake in the bottom of the oven for 45 to 50 minutes. Spoon out the portions of apple pie and serve with some custard!

CALORIES	FAT	SAT FAT	PROTEIN	CARBS	SUGAR	SALT	FIBRE
482kcal	22.6g	13.2g	5.6g	68.2g	38g	0g	3g

ROAST CHICKEN WITH LEMON & ROSEMARY ROAST POTATOES

Roast chicken remains one of our favourite dishes at home, so that's why I've included it in The Top Ten. I recently discovered a way to make the chicken taste even better, by putting a lemon in with my potatoes when parboiling them. It smelt fantastic and flavoured the potatoes, then when I was draining them I decided to stab the lemon, which hissed out juice and steam, and quickly jammed it inside the chicken! The benefits of the hot steaming lemon are very obvious as the meat tastes amazing, and the chicken cooks slightly more quickly because of it.

SERVES 6
1 x 2kg whole chicken
1.5kg potatoes, peeled
1 large lemon
1 whole bulb of garlic, broken into cloves
1 bunch of fresh thyme
olive oil
1 bunch of fresh rosemary, leaves picked
optional: 8 rashers of smoked streaky bacon

In the morning, rub the chicken inside and out with a generous amount of sea salt and black pepper, then cover and leave in the fridge until you're ready to cook. Preheat the oven to 190°C/375°F/gas 5. Cut the potatoes into golf-ball-sized pieces, and cook them in a pan of boiling salted water with the whole lemon and the garlic cloves for 12 minutes. Drain and allow to steam dry for 1 minute (this will give you crispier potatoes), then remove the lemon and garlic. Toss the potatoes in the pan while still hot so their outsides get chuffed up and fluffy – this will make them lovely and crispy when they roast.

While the lemon is still hot, carefully stab it about 10 times. Take the chicken out of the fridge, pat it with kitchen paper and rub it all over with oil. Push the garlic cloves, the whole lemon and the thyme into the cavity, then put the chicken into a roasting tray and roast for 45 minutes. Remove the chicken to a plate. Some lovely fat should have cooked out of it into the roasting tray, so toss the potatoes into this with the rosemary leaves. Shake the tray around, then make a gap in the centre of the potatoes and put the chicken back in. Lay the bacon over the chicken breast (if using) and cook for a further 45 minutes, or until the potatoes are golden and the thigh meat pulls easily away from the bone and the juices run clear.

I like to remove the bacon from the chicken and crumble it up over the potatoes, then I remove the lemon, garlic and thyme from the cavity, squeeze all the garlic flesh out of the skin, mush it up and spread it all over the chicken, discard the lemon and carve the chicken at the table. Heaven!

CALORIES	FAT	SAT FAT	PROTEIN	CARBS	SUGAR	SALT	FIBRE
496kcal	16.8g	4.7g	44.6g	44.1g	1.6g	1.6g	3.5g

FISH, CHIPS & MUSHY PEAS

Good fish and chips are becoming harder to find these days, so if you want to make your own at home, here's the recipe I use. Unless you've got a really big fryer I'd say it's not really worth trying to make fish and chips at home for more than 4 people – otherwise it becomes a struggle. Other things to have on the table are some crunchy sweet pickled gherkins, some pickled onions (if your other half isn't around!) – and pickled chillies are good, too. Douse it all with some malt vinegar and tomato ketchup. Delicious!

SERVES 4

sunflower oil, for frying
4 x 225g nice white fish fillets,
   pin-boned
225g flour, plus extra for dusting
300ml cold beer
3 heaped teaspoons baking
   powder
1kg potatoes, peeled and
   sliced into chips

MUSHY PEAS

1 knob of unsalted butter
4 handfuls of podded peas
½ a bunch of fresh mint, leaves picked
   and chopped
½ a lemon

Preheat the oven to 180°C/350°F/gas 4. To make the mushy peas, put the butter in a pan with the peas and the chopped mint. Put a lid on top and simmer for about 10 minutes. Add a squeeze of lemon juice and season with sea salt and black pepper. You can either mush the peas up in a food processor, or you can mash them by hand until they are stodgy, thick and perfect for dipping your fish into. Keep them warm while you cook the fish and chips.

Pour sunflower oil into a deep fat fryer or a sturdy pan and heat it to 190°C. Mix ½ a teaspoon of salt and ½ a teaspoon of pepper together and season the fish fillets on both sides – this will help to remove any excess water, making the fish really meaty. Whisk the flour, beer and baking powder together until thick enough to stick to whatever you're coating. Dust each fillet in a little of the extra flour, then dip into the batter and allow any excess to drip off. Holding one end, carefully lower the fish into the oil one by one, so you don't get splashed – it will depend on the size of your fryer how many fish you can do at once. Cook for 4 minutes, or until golden and crisp.

Meanwhile, parboil the chips in boiling salted water for about 4 or 5 minutes, or until softened but still retaining their shape, then drain them in a colander and leave to steam completely dry. When all the moisture has disappeared, fry them in the oil that the fish were cooked in at 180°C until golden and crisp. While the chips are frying, place the fish on a baking tray in the oven for a few minutes to finish cooking. When the chips are done, drain them on kitchen paper, season with salt, and serve with the fish and mushy peas.

CALORIES	FAT	SAT FAT	PROTEIN	CARBS	SUGAR	SALT	FIBRE
980kcal	43.7g	7.3g	54.5g	94g	4.8g	3g	6.4g

THE BEST CHICKEN & SWEET LEEK PIE WITH FLAKY PASTRY

I've always loved chicken pie. Apart from being quick, simple and scrumptious, puff pastry gives you a really flaky, crispy top, which I can never get enough of. I was invited to dinner at the food critic Fay Maschler's home a while back and she made me a wonderful chicken pie. Her tip was to put some sausagemeat balls in the stew and they tasted fantastic. Three stars!

SERVES 6

olive oil
2 knobs of unsalted butter
1kg chicken thighs, skin off, bone out,
    cut into pieces
2 medium leeks, trimmed, washed and
    sliced into 1cm pieces
2 carrots, peeled and roughly chopped
3 sticks of celery, finely sliced

½ a bunch of fresh thyme, leaves picked
2 tablespoons plain flour
1 wineglass of white wine
300ml milk
250g pork sausages
500g all-butter puff pastry
1 large egg

Preheat the oven to 220°C/425°F/gas 7. Drizzle a lug of oil into a large casserole pan, then add the butter, chicken, leeks, carrots, celery and thyme. Cook slowly on the hob for 15 minutes, stirring occasionally. Turn the heat right up, add the flour, and keep stirring for a couple of minutes before adding the wine, a wineglass of water and the milk. Season with a little sea salt and black pepper, then cover with a lid and simmer very slowly on the hob for 30 to 40 minutes, or until the chicken is tender, stirring occasionally. The sauce should be loose but quite thick – if it's a little too liquidy, continue to simmer it with the lid off until it thickens slightly. At this point you could let it cool and keep it in the fridge for up to 2 days – it can also be eaten as a stew.

Pour the chicken mixture into a pie dish. Squeeze the meat out of the sausage skins, roll it into little balls, brown them in a little oil and sprinkle them over the stew. Roll out the pastry to about ½cm thick. Eggwash the rim of the dish and drape over the pastry, using a knife to trim the edge of the dish. Eggwash the top of the pastry to make it go golden while cooking, then pinch it to crimp it round the edges (there's no need to do this, but I like to as my mum always does it and it makes it look pretty). I use the back of a knife to lightly criss-cross the top – this allows the pastry to go crisp and flaky. Cook the pie in the centre of the oven for about 30 to 40 minutes, or until golden. I like to serve this with sweetcorn and mashed potato.

CALORIES	FAT	SAT FAT	PROTEIN	CARBS	SUGAR	SALT	FIBRE
715kcal	38.6g	16.7g	51.6g	37.6g	8.1g	2g	4.1g

TOMATO SOUP

I've made all sorts of different tomato soups over the years, and this is probably one of the simplest and tastiest. Here's the trick ... if you go down to your local market at the end of the day, you may find they are selling off tomatoes cheap. More than likely the seller thinks they are over-ripe, but they are more probably just perfect and will make great soup. If you can't get these, buy tomatoes two or three days before you need them, but don't keep them in the fridge as they won't ripen. Leave them on a windowsill to get ripe. If there's a choice, then have a taste – you'll be amazed how different they can be, so choose the ones that taste the best. The second trick is the slow cooking, which makes them very sweet. Best served in warm bowls or mugs at the table with some really fresh bread.

SERVES 4
1 onion, peeled and finely chopped
1 clove of garlic, peeled and finely chopped
1 carrot, peeled and coarsely grated
1 bunch of fresh basil, leaves picked, stalks finely chopped
olive oil
6 tablespoons double cream
1 teaspoon red wine vinegar
2 large egg yolks
1kg super-ripe tomatoes
1 litre quality chicken or vegetable stock

Put the onion, garlic, carrot and basil stalks into a large pan with a couple of lugs of oil. Cover and simmer gently without colouring for 20 minutes, stirring every couple of minutes. Whisk the cream, vinegar and egg yolks together in a small bowl and put to one side. While the veg are simmering, drop the tomatoes into boiling water for 30 seconds, then remove the skins and roughly chop the flesh. Add this to the veg, then pour in the stock and simmer for a further 20 minutes with the lid on. At this point it's nice to purée the soup using either a food processor, a blender or a stick blender, but be careful as it will be hot. Once you've puréed the soup, put it back into the pan, bring it back to a simmer, and season carefully with sea salt and black pepper.

Just before serving, to enrich the soup and give it a shine and silky texture, whisk in the cream mixture (don't reboil it after adding the egg yolks or it will scramble) and serve straight away, sprinkled with a few extra torn-up basil leaves if you like.

CALORIES	FAT	SAT FAT	PROTEIN	CARBS	SUGAR	SALT	FIBRE
252kcal	19.8g	8.8g	5.2g	13.9g	12.5g	0.6g	4.6g

CHICKEN TIKKA MASALA

This is a really popular curry dish which loads of people order from their local curry houses at the weekend. If you've ever thought of making it at home, you may have been slightly mystified about how to make it taste so good, but have a go at this recipe and I'm sure you won't be disappointed. The great thing about it is that if you don't fancy chicken you can try using lamb instead, because it's cooked separately from the sauce.

SERVES 4

6 cloves of garlic, peeled
7.5cm piece of ginger, peeled
2–3 fresh red chillies, deseeded
olive oil
1 tablespoon mustard seeds
1 tablespoon smoked paprika
2 teaspoons ground cumin
2 teaspoons ground coriander
3 tablespoons garam masala
200g natural yoghurt

4 x 120g skinless chicken breasts, cut into large chunks
1 tablespoon unsalted butter
2 medium onions, peeled and finely sliced
2 tablespoons tomato purée
1 small handful of ground unsalted cashew nuts or almonds
50ml single cream
1 handful of fresh coriander, chopped
1–2 limes

Grate the garlic and ginger on the finest side of a cheese grater and put to one side in a bowl. Chop the chillies as finely as you can and mix them in with the ginger and garlic. Drizzle a good splash of oil into a pan and add the mustard seeds. When they start to pop, add them to the ginger and garlic mixture along with the paprika, cumin, ground coriander and 2 tablespoons of the garam masala. Put half into a bowl, add the yoghurt and the chicken pieces then toss to coat and leave to marinate for at least 30 minutes, preferably longer.

Melt the butter in the pan the mustard seeds were in and add the sliced onions and the remaining spice mix. Cook gently for 15 minutes, or until softened – it should start to smell fantastic! Add the tomato purée, the ground nuts, 500ml of water and ½ a teaspoon of sea salt. Stir well and simmer gently for a few minutes, or until slightly thickened and reduced.

Put the marinated chicken on to a hot griddle or barbecue and sear until cooked through – you can also do this under the grill if you like.

Warm the sauce, add the cream and the remaining tablespoon of garam masala. Taste and correct the seasoning, if needed. As soon as it boils, take off the heat and add the grilled chicken. Scatter over the chopped coriander and squeeze over the lime juice. Delicious served with a huge bowl of steaming basmati rice, some poppadoms and lots of cold beer!

CALORIES	FAT	SAT FAT	PROTEIN	CARBS	SUGAR	SALT	FIBRE
225kcal	8.5g	2.7g	27.5g	10.4g	8.6g	0.3g	1.8g

TAKE AN IDEA

TAKE ONE CORE PRINCIPLE

FAMILY

PUFF PASTRY

ALL BUTTER

FRESH — FROZEN

PARMESAN TWISTS

BASHED FENNEL SEEDS

JAM

SUGAR

APPLES — PEARS

7" plate!

ICE CREAM — CRÈME FRAÎCHE

JAMMY
QUICK JAMME
APPLE TART

CUMBERLAND SAUSAGE ROLLS

CHEDDAR CHEESE

EGG WASH

ROSEMARY

THYME

SAGE

SQUASH
A CHERRY TOMATO

MINI CALZONES
WITH PROSCIUTTO
MOZZARELLA AND
TOMATO

BRANSTON PICKLE

FLO

ROCKE
SAL

FRESH? — JAR? — FOOD PROCESSOR? — PESTLE + MORTAR?

OLIVE OIL

PINE NUTS

PESTO

BASIL

CREAMINESS

CIABATTA

1kg

BRUISE NOT CHOP

PASTA WITH PESTO

LEMON

FRESH ROSEMARY LEAVES

GREEN SALAD

PESTO WITH ROASTED CHICKEN

POTATOES

COURGETTES — LEEKS

PESTO DIP

FENNEL

GREEN BASIL

PURPLE BASIL

MUSSELS WITH PESTO

ROASTED VEG

CARROTS

POTATOES

COD — GREEN SALAD

FISH WITH PESTO

CHARDONNAY

BRUSCHETTA

RUB WITH GARLIC

BEEF

OLIVE OIL

PESTO WITH
TOMATO SALAD

CHERRY

PESTO WITH VEG KEBABS

RED ONION — MUSHROOMS

VINE

BASIL LEAVES

PESTO WITH MOZZARELLA

ROSEMARY STICKS — COURGETTES

TREE

learn one recipe

CREATE SOMETHING DIFFERENT

FREEZE — OLIVE OIL — CHILLI

GARLIC — RED WINE VINEGAR

MUSH — TWANG

DON'T CHOP

ITALIAN — BASIL

TINNED

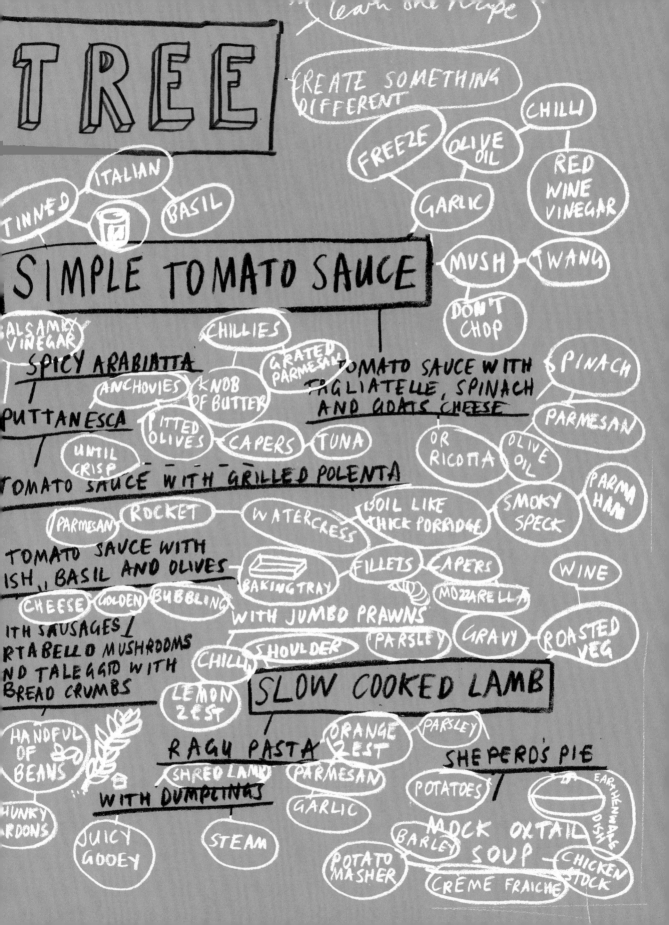

SIMPLE TOMATO SAUCE

BALSAMIC VINEGAR

SPICY ARABIATTA

CHILLIES

GRATED PARMESAN

TOMATO SAUCE WITH TAGLIATELLE, SPINACH AND GOATS CHEESE — SPINACH — PARMESAN

PUTTANESCA

ANCHOVIES — KNOB OF BUTTER

PITTED OLIVES — CAPERS — TUNA

UNTIL CRISP

OR RICOTTA — OLIVE OIL

PARMA HAM

TOMATO SAUCE WITH GRILLED POLENTA

PARMESAN — ROCKET — WATERCRESS — BOIL LIKE THICK PORRIDGE — SMOKY SPECK

TOMATO SAUCE WITH FISH, BASIL AND OLIVES

BAKING TRAY — FILLETS — CAPERS — WINE

MOZZARELLA

CHEESE — GOLDEN — BUBBLING

WITH JUMBO PRAWNS

WITH SAUSAGES / PORTABELLO MUSHROOMS AND TALEGGIO WITH BREAD CRUMBS

SHOULDER — PARSLEY — GRAVY — ROASTED VEG

CHILLI

LEMON ZEST

SLOW COOKED LAMB

HANDFUL OF BEANS

RAGU PASTA

ORANGE ZEST — PARSLEY

SHEPERD'S PIE

POTATOES

EARTHENWARE DISH

SHRED LAMB — PARMESAN

WITH DUMPLINGS

GARLIC

HUNKY CARDONS

JUICY GOOEY — STEAM

MOCK OXTAIL SOUP

BARLEY — CHICKEN STOCK

POTATO MASHER — CRÈME FRAICHE

I've called this chapter 'Family Tree' because once you've perfected one really good 'parent' recipe, you can make lots of 'offspring' recipes. It's a chapter for nervous or novice cooks, and it should give you the confidence to think, 'I'm the boss, I'm in control and I'm going to cook an amazing meal tonight, and the next night, and the next . . . !'

Many years ago I worked with a waiter called Angus who never cooked. Between services one day he was helping out by picking the basil for me to make fresh pesto. He'd seen me make it a few times and wanted to have a go himself, so I taught him how to do it. 'Unbelievable!' he said. 'That's so easy, even an idiot could do it!'

This was around the time of the World Cup, so he had all the boys round to his house for a few bevvies and some food. He told me afterwards that he put a packet of pasta on to boil, bashed up the basil, then added the pine nuts and cheese to make the pesto. He made it with complete ease, and plonked it down in front of his (very!) impressed mates, who wasted no time tucking in with gusto. For weeks after that they were all saying what a great cook Angus was. Then he came over to me one day and told me he'd had his girlfriend and family over. He'd roasted a chicken, served a green salad out of a packet, dressed with a little bit of oil and vinegar, and then made the pesto at the table and served it with the chicken – his parents were amazed! They couldn't believe how independent their son had become and how tasty the food was!

So this chapter is all about showing you how you can learn one recipe, and then use it to champion a whole set of different meals while fooling everyone into believing you're the best cook in the world! Being a cook is about ducking and diving your way around dishes. I just love the fact that I can take an idea and move it on in some small way to create my own customized recipes. After you've had a look through this chapter, have a go at coming up with your own ideas or ways of doing things.

Some of the recipes in this chapter haven't got lists of ingredients because I wanted them to be chatty. I also feel that sometimes it's important to read the whole recipe through before you start, to get more of an understanding of how the whole thing works. Instead I have highlighted the ingredients so you can see, at a glance, what you'll need.

PESTO

First I'm going to show you an easy recipe for making pesto, then I'll give you some ideas on how best to use it, instead of just having it with pasta all the time. When it comes to making pesto, you can invest in a food processor if you like, but you can also make it using a pestle and mortar. If you have a blunt blade from your processor, then don't chuck it, but keep it specially for making pesto or marinades where you need to bruise out the flavour, instead of chopping. You may think it's nice to toast the pine nuts until they're coloured, to give them a nutty taste, but the really good pestos I've tasted in Italy have them just very lightly toasted, to give a creaminess rather than a nuttiness. Pesto is normally made with green basil, but purple basil looks good if you can get hold of some. Another way, slightly more American, uses rocket instead of basil – it's fragrant and interesting with roasted meats, but I prefer this classic pesto recipe.

SERVES 4
½ a clove of garlic, peeled and chopped
1 big bunch of fresh basil (60g), leaves picked and chopped
1 handful of pine nuts, very lightly toasted
1 good handful of freshly grated Parmesan cheese
extra virgin olive oil
optional: ½ a lemon

Pound the garlic with a little pinch of sea salt and the basil leaves in a pestle and mortar, or pulse in a food processor. Add a bit more garlic if you like, but I usually stick to ½ a clove. Throw in the pine nuts and pound again. Turn out into a bowl and add half the Parmesan, then stir gently and add oil – you need just enough to bind the sauce and get it to an oozy consistency.

Season to taste with sea salt and black pepper, then add most of the remaining cheese. Pour in some more oil and taste again. Keep adding a bit more cheese or oil until you are happy with the taste and consistency. You may like to add a squeeze of lemon juice at the end to give it a little twang, but it's not essential. Try it with and without and see which you prefer.

CALORIES	FAT	SAT FAT	PROTEIN	CARBS	SUGAR	SALT	FIBRE
221kcal	22.3g	3.9g	4.3g	0.9g	0.5g	0.4g	0.3g

PESTO

with Roasted Chicken
For 6 people get yourself a 2kg **chicken**. Preheat the oven to 220°C/425°F/gas 7. Parboil 1.5kg of **potatoes** with a whole **lemon** in the water to give some flavour. Drain the spuds, then remove the lemon and prick it with a knife a few times before pushing it inside the chicken. Bash up a handful of fresh **rosemary leaves,** drizzle them with **olive oil** and stuff them into the chicken as well. Roast the chicken for 30 minutes, then throw the parboiled potatoes into the tray and roast for 1 hour, or until the chicken is cooked through and the potatoes are golden. I really like to make the **pesto** at the table – it only takes 4 minutes if you've got everything ready. Serve the pesto with the chicken and the lovely roast potatoes, and maybe with some ciabatta bread, a big green salad and some beers.

with Mussels
This is a creamy mussel dish which is a little bit like the French way of serving mussels with a garlicky sauce. When you put pesto with garlic into a broth or soup it really makes the room smell amazing as it hits the warmth. For 6 people get 1.8kg of nice **mussels,** chuck away any open shells and debeard the rest if needed. By this I mean pull off the little scruffy 'beards' which hang out of the shells. Get yourself a large pot, heat it up, add a couple of lugs of **olive oil** and fry a peeled and finely chopped **onion,** 3 or 4 peeled and chopped cloves of **garlic** and a little deseeded and finely chopped **fresh chilli.** Throw the mussels in with one glass of **white wine** and 75ml of **single cream.** Put a lid on top and simmer for 10 minutes, or until the shells have opened. Discard any that remain closed. Add a knob of unsalted **butter** and give the pan a little shake. The mussels should be really soft and tender. Correct the seasoning with a little **sea salt and black pepper** – though you might not need salt – and a squeeze of **lemon juice.** Serve in a big bowl with all the juices and ½ a bunch of chopped fresh **flat-leaf parsley or basil** sprinkled over. Serve the **pesto** spooned over the top. Really nice with a warm baguette.

with Bruschetta
When your mates turn up for a barbecue and are having a few beers while they wait for their food, just toast some slices of **ciabatta,** rub with the cut side of a **garlic clove,** then spoon over some **pesto** and finish with a drizzle of **extra virgin olive oil.**

with Fish
Get yourself a **fillet of nice white fish,** such as **cod,** and rub it with **olive oil.** Season it with **sea salt and black pepper,** then either grill or pan-fry and serve with a nice big spoonful of **pesto** over the top. On the side, have a green salad and a nice glass of white wine.

PESTO

with Mixed Tomato Salad
Get yourself some different varieties of tomato – little cherry ones, big beef ones or ones on the vine – and slice them all up. Lay them on a plate with some basil leaves torn over, a drizzle of extra virgin olive oil, some sea salt and black pepper and a big dollop of pesto. You could even stir this tomato salad through some hot, drained pasta.

with Roasted Vegetables
Preheat the oven to 190°C/375°F/gas 5. There are so many combinations of vegetables that can be roasted well together: carrots, squash, parsnips, turnips, potatoes, celeriac, swede, fennel and red onions. All you need to do is cut them into similar-sized chunks and roast them all together, in the same roasting tray, in a little olive oil with some sea salt and black pepper for 45 minutes, or until golden. Mix all the veg together and serve with a little bowl of pesto – lovely. If you want to make these part of a more substantial dinner, roast a leg of lamb to go with them, but either way these veggies are fantastic served as a starter, a vegetable dish or an accompaniment to meat or fish.

with Vegetable Kebabs
These kebabs are lovely cooked on the barbecue, but are just as easily done under the grill. Get yourself a selection of veggies – try aubergine, mushrooms, peppers, red onion and courgettes. Dice them into pieces roughly the same size and spear them on to some rosemary sticks or skewers. Drizzle over some olive oil, season with sea salt and black pepper, and grill or barbecue for 5 to 10 minutes, or until soft and nicely cooked. Serve with the pesto.

with Mozzarella
Get yourself a nice ball of buffalo mozzarella cheese, tear it up, and eat it with pesto as a great starter. Lovely served with some roasted peppers, ciabatta and fresh basil or wild rocket.

SIMPLE TOMATO SAUCE

SERVES 4

I'm a great believer in a simple tomato sauce, but it has to be made properly. The quality of the tinned tomatoes is important, and the only way to tell the difference between good ones and great ones is to try out a few varieties. I've recently come across an Italian brand called La Fiammante. Each tin contains one basil leaf to flavour the tomatoes and they taste superb. I find it's more economical to make one big batch of tomato sauce every so often – I divide it up into sandwich bags and pop them into the freezer for another day or into the fridge for up to a week.

First of all, chop 2 or 3 cloves of **garlic** and fry them gently in **olive oil** with either some chopped **basil stalks** or a good pinch of **dried oregano,** and a whole **fresh red chilli.** Pierce the chilli once with a knife so it doesn't explode when frying – it will give a subtle heat to the sauce. Add a couple of **tins of quality plum tomatoes** – try to get hold of the best Italian ones you can – and leave the tomatoes whole. The seeds can be a little bitter, so if you chop the tomatoes up straight away, the sauce won't be as sweet as it should be. Lightly season with **sea salt and black pepper,** then gently simmer for 30 minutes. Remove the chilli.

Break up the tomatoes up with the back of a spoon, season the sauce really carefully with more salt and pepper, and add a tiny swig of **red wine vinegar** to give it a little twang. It should now be perfect! There are so many different ways you can take this sauce forward …

CALORIES	FAT	SAT FAT	PROTEIN	CARBS	SUGAR	SALT	FIBRE
42kcal	0.3g	0g	2.5g	8.1g	7.6g	0.5g	1.7g

PASTA SAUCES

- For a spicy arrabiatta, start the tomato sauce off by adding a few more whole **fresh red chillies.** After the sauce has simmered for 15 to 20 minutes, remove the chillies, chop them up and add back as much as you need to give your arrabiatta the desired heat. One of my favourites.

- A real crowd-pleaser can be made by taking the tomato sauce off the heat when it's ready and adding a big handful of torn fresh **basil,** a nice swig of **balsamic vinegar,** a good knob of **unsalted butter** and a handful of grated **Parmesan cheese.** This is fantastic with pasta like rigatoni or tagliatelle, or with grilled meats and fish.

- To make a puttanesca, simmer the sauce gently with a handful of good pitted and squashed **olives,** a couple of **anchovy fillets,** in oil (drained) and a handful of **capers.** You can take this in a different direction by flaking in a **tin of tuna** in spring water (drained) when the sauce is ready.

TOMATO SAUCE

with Tagliatelle, Spinach & Goat's Cheese
Once I've made my basic **tomato sauce,** this is one of my favourite ways to turn it into a desirable pasta dish. Simmer it in a large pan while you cook some **tagliatelle** in boiling salted water according to the packet instructions. Just before the pasta is ready, add a large handful of **baby spinach** to the sauce and check the seasoning. Drain the pasta, saving a little of the cooking water, then toss with a little **olive oil** and some of the reserved water to loosen it, and pour the sauce over the top. Toss again. Divide between plates, sprinkle over some freshly grated **Parmesan cheese** and crumble over some **goat's cheese.** You can also try using crumbled feta or ricotta – you'll love it.

with Grilled Polenta You can use your tomato sauce as a posh version of ketchup to serve with grilled chicken or white fish. Or even with polenta – here's an easy recipe. Boil your **coarse polenta** according to the packet instructions, stirring all the time, until you have a stodgy consistency like thick porridge. Season with **sea salt and black pepper,** add a little knob of **unsalted butter** and some freshly grated **Parmesan cheese,** then pour the polenta out on to an oiled baking tray so it's about 2.5cm thick. Leave to cool and set – between 1 and 2 hours – then grill in slices until crisp. Serve with some **tomato sauce** spooned over the top, and a little bunch of dressed **watercress or rocket** wrapped up in some smoky **speck or Parma ham.** Shave over some Parmesan, using a speed-peeler, and finish with a drizzle of **extra virgin olive oil.**

TOMATO SAUCE

with Fish, Olives & Basil
Warm the **tomato sauce** in an ovenproof pan and put a couple of **fish fillets** on top. If you prefer to use chicken breasts, brown them first in a little oil before placing on top. Sprinkle with some destoned **olives, baby capers and fresh basil** and, if you have any to hand, a little torn **mozzarella cheese.** Bake in the oven at 220°C/425°F/gas 7 for 15 minutes, or until the fish is just cooked. If using chicken breasts, they will need around 20 minutes.

with Portobello Mushrooms & Taleggio
Pour the warmed **tomato sauce** into a small baking dish and place some nice **Portobello or field mushrooms,** with the stalks facing up, on top. Slice over some **Taleggio** – this is a lovely melting cheese and it's beautiful with these mushrooms – and sprinkle over some fresh **thyme leaves.** You could even scatter over some **breadcrumbs,** drizzled with **olive oil.** Bake in the oven at 220°C/425°F/gas 7 for 15 to 20 minutes, or until golden.

with Sausages
Pour the warmed **tomato sauce** into a baking dish. Get yourself some nice **sausages** and toss them in a little **olive oil,** then place on top of the sauce and cook at 220°C/425°F/gas 7 for about 30 minutes, or until the sausages are cooked through. It will be almost like a cassoulet – the sausages will be soft and juicy on the bottom from the sauce, and lovely and crisp on top. On the cassoulet vibe, a **tin of beans, such as cannellini, flageolet, haricot or chickpeas,** or chunky lardons of **smoked bacon** added to this would be fantastic.

with Marinated Jumbo Prawns
Ask your fishmonger to remove the shells from a couple of handfuls of **large raw king prawns,** then when you get home all you have to do is run a knife down the back of each one to remove the little black vein. Squeeze over some **lemon juice,** drizzle with **olive oil,** and scatter over chopped **fresh flat-leaf parsley** and chopped **fresh red chilli.** Leave to marinate for at least 5 minutes and up to an hour. Put the **tomato sauce** into a pan and sprinkle in the prawns and their marinating juices. Put the lid on and either slowly simmer on the hob or roast for just 5 minutes at 220°C/425°F/gas 7. Serve with grilled ciabatta and a nice chilled bottle of white wine – makes a great starter. You could even chuck a handful of mussels or clams in with the prawns, or try having the sauce with a whole lobster cut in half.

SLOW-COOKED SHOULDER OF LAMB
WITH ROASTED VEGETABLES

This is a recipe that I first made as an alternative to roasting a leg of lamb. I wanted to save time and make my own gravy, so I turned it into a pot roast by adding vegetables and wine. I think shoulder of lamb is one of the best cuts by far – it's tastier than leg and much more economical. I've taken it in various different directions and come up with some fantastic Family Tree ideas …

SERVES 8
1 x 2.25kg shoulder of lamb, bone in
olive oil
1 bunch of fresh rosemary
1 whole bulb of garlic, broken into cloves
2 red onions, peeled and quartered
3 carrots, peeled and roughly chopped
2 sticks of celery, cut into pieces
1 large leek or 2–3 baby leeks, trimmed, washed and cut into pieces
1 handful of ripe tomatoes, halved
2 fresh bay leaves
½ a bunch of fresh thyme
2 x 400g tins of quality plum tomatoes
1 bottle of red wine

Preheat the oven to 200°C/400°F/gas 6. Rub the lamb with oil, sea salt and black pepper and put it into a roasting tray. Using a sharp knife, make small incisions all over the lamb and poke rosemary leaves and some peeled and quartered cloves of garlic into each one – this will give great flavour to the meat. Add the rest of the unpeeled garlic cloves, the onions, carrots, celery, leeks and fresh tomatoes to the tray, then tuck the remaining herbs under the meat. Pour the tinned tomatoes over the top, followed by the wine. Cover the tray tightly with a double layer of tin foil and place in the oven. Turn down the oven temperature down to 170°C/325°F/gas 3 and cook for 3 hours and 30 minutes to 4 hours, or until meltingly tender. Gently break up the meat, pull out the bones, and discard any herb stalks. Squeeze the garlic out of the skins and mush it in. Shred the lamb and season to taste. Delicious served with roast potatoes.

CALORIES	FAT	SAT FAT	PROTEIN	CARBS	SUGAR	SALT	FIBRE
462kcal	26.2g	12g	30.2g	11.2g	8.8g	0.8g	2.8g

SLOW-COOKED LAMB

Ragù Pasta Using the slow-cooked lamb for this recipe makes it far closer to an original ragù dish than if you use mince. I think you'll really love it. If you happen to have the zest from an **orange,** some chopped **fresh flat-leaf parsley** and a peeled and chopped clove of **garlic,** mix them together and try sprinkling over the top of the pasta just before serving – it will give an incredible flavour. Cook some **spaghetti or tagliatelle** – 450g for 6 people – in boiling salted water according to the packet instructions, then drain, reserving a little cooking water. Stir the shredded **lamb** through your pasta and add a good handful of freshly grated **Parmesan cheese.** Loosen with a splash of cooking water, if needed, then serve in large bowls.

with My Mum's Dumplings This recipe is really simple. Preheat the oven to 190°C/375°F/gas 5, then stir the following ingredients together in a bowl: 225g of **self-raising flour,** 100g of **unsalted butter or suet,** a handful of chopped **fresh rosemary, thyme or flat-leaf parsley,** 30g of grated **Cheddar or Gruyère cheese** and ½ a level teaspoon of **sea salt.** Slowly add 140ml of cold water and mix until the dough binds together. Divide into 8 pieces and roll them into golf-ball-sized dumplings. Once the **lamb** is cooked and shredded, put it into a pan and warm gently – you may need to add a little water to thin the sauce out. Lay the dumplings on top of the stew (or dunk them under if you prefer – this will make them glossy and dark when cooked), then, if your pan is ovenproof, put it into the oven for 40 minutes, covering the pan for the first 25 minutes. Or put a tight-fitting lid on the pan and finish it on top of the stove so the dumplings can steam, for 1 hour. Either way, the dumplings will suck up loads of the fantastic cooking juices, leaving you with nice, firm, tasty meat and juicy, gooey dumplings.

Shepherd's Pie Once the **lamb** is cooked and shredded, transfer it to a casserole pan or baking dish that will allow the meat to sit about 2.5cm deep. Cover with **mashed potato,** add a sprig of fresh **rosemary** and bake in the oven at 200°C/400°F/gas 6 for 35 minutes, or until golden.

STEWED FRUIT

I know what you're thinking … stewed fruit = school dinners = not very exciting. But I'm here to change your mind – stewing, or gently poaching, fruit is a fantastic way of altering your perceived flavour of it. When stewed together with a little sugar and water (or maybe some alcohol like wine, port, brandy, rum or sherry) and other spices or flavourings, all types of fruit can take on a whole different vibe. Try a cinnamon stick or almonds with apricots and peaches, a couple of cloves with apples and pears, five-spice with plums, vanilla and orange zest with rhubarb (lemon zest and ginger are both good, too!). But the one thing you have to remember is to try to keep as much of the fruit's shape and colour as you can, otherwise you'll end up with a jammy liquid.

Use any of the following fruits, depending on what's in season: rhubarb, peaches, pears, strawberries, plums, apples, cherries, figs, gooseberries, blackberries and blackcurrants. Now I would say stewed fruit is starting to sound a bit sexier! The other brilliant thing is that this dish can be made very cheaply and can be easily transformed down the Family Tree, as you'll see.

SERVES 8

1 vanilla pod
200g caster sugar
optional: 1 clove
optional: ¼ of a stick of cinnamon
1 star anise
¼ of an orange
2 pears, each peeled and cut into eight
4 peaches, halved and destoned

4 plums, halved and destoned
500g rhubarb trimmed and roughly
   chopped into chunky pieces
1 handful of strawberries, hulled
1 handful of blackberries
optional: ½ a bunch of fresh basil
   or mint, leaves picked

Halve the vanilla pod lengthways and scrape out the seeds. Put the sugar and 250ml of water into a pot on the heat, and when it starts to warm up add the vanilla pod and seeds, the clove, and cinnamon stick (if using), the star anise, and grate in the orange zest. Bring to the boil until the liquid becomes clear, then remove the clove, cinnamon and star anise. Reduce to a simmer and put the firmer fruit into the pot – in this case, the pears and peaches, followed by the plums and rhubarb a few minutes later. Simmer slowly for 5 or 6 minutes, or until tender. A couple of minutes before the end, add the strawberries and blackberries. Let the fruit sit in the syrup for all the flavours to develop. If serving just as fruit with its flavoured syrup and ice cream, don't overcook it to keep it fresh, light and colourful. However, if I want a pulp, I will remove the lid and continue to cook it, stirring as often as I can.

Divide the fruit between bowls, spoon over the hot syrup and finish by sprinkling over some fresh basil or mint leaves (if using). Delicious with a dollop of cream.

CALORIES	FAT	SAT FAT	PROTEIN	CARBS	SUGAR	SALT	FIBRE
142kcal	0.2g	0g	1.2g	36.3g	36.3g	0g	2.1g

STEWED FRUIT

Crumble If you want to turn the **stewed fruit** into a crumble for 6, divide it between 6 ovenproof bowls. Top with a crumble mixture made by rubbing together 225g of **plain flour,** 100g of **unsalted butter,** 100g of **sugar** and a pinch of **sea salt.** Sprinkle the mixture over the fruit and bake in the oven at 180°C/350°F/gas 4 for 15 to 20 minutes, or until the top is crisp and the fruit is bubbling up at the sides. You can always make one large crumble, if you prefer.

Syllabub Syllabubs date back to the sixteenth century and are lovely cold desserts – they are made with cream and can be flavoured with sugar, wine or lemon juice. Stewed fruit is also a perfect flavouring. All you have to do is whip **double cream** to form soft peaks and, when it's nice and thick, pour the **stewed fruit** on to it and mix together (delicious made with yoghurt, too). Serve in small individual glasses or bowls, with a little grated **orange zest** sprinkled over the top.

on Toast Stewed fruit is lovely with toast, although you may think it sounds a bit strange! All you have to do to make this simple dessert is spread some **unsalted butter** on some nice **toasted bread,** then spread over the **stewed fruit,** crumble over some **ricotta or nice goat's cheese** and drizzle lightly with **runny honey.**

Filo Pastry Parcels Buy a packet of **filo pastry** sheets, then all you have to do is keep the pile of them underneath a damp cloth while you work with 2 sheets at a time. Take 2 sheets and brush them with melted **unsalted butter,** then stick them together. Cut into a square 20cm x 20cm and spoon 2 tablespoons of the **stewed fruit** into the middle of the square. Crumble over a little **ricotta cheese** and sprinkle over some **muscovado sugar,** then bring the sides of the filo pastry up and squeeze them together to make a little parcel. Brush the top with melted butter and place on a baking tray. Repeat with the rest of the filo sheets and stewed fruit. Bake in the oven at 170°C/325°F/gas 3 for 15 to 20 minutes, or until golden and crisp.

with Yoghurt Stewed fruit is also really nice with a spoonful of **natural yoghurt,** some **runny honey** and a scattering of **porridge oats.**

PUFF PASTRY

Frozen, pre-made puff pastry is available just about everywhere. Unlike shortcrust, which is quite easy to make yourself, puff is a real palaver unless you've got loads of time. So I would advise that you buy it, and the all-butter puff pastry is the one to look for. For those of you who aren't sure what puff pastry is, it's a type of pastry that has butter folded into it and is then rolled and folded with many layers, so that when it cooks it expands and you get the millefeuille effect, as the French call it (this means 'thousand-leaf', because this is what it looks like with all its layers). It looks great when it's all puffed up, and it has a fantastic crispy and chewy texture. Great for desserts, to go on pies and stews, stuff like that. Here are some Family Tree ideas for puff pastry ...

Parmesan Twists
One of the quickest and easiest things to do with puff pastry is to make these little 'twists' to have as munchies, to eat with salad or with drinks at a dinner party. These can be made, then frozen (uncooked) for when you have unexpected guests. On a floured surface, roll out the **puff pastry** to ½cm thick. Brush the surface with a little beaten **egg.** Sprinkle over a pinch of **smoked paprika** (or try poppy seeds, sesame seeds or bashed fennel seeds), and cut across the width into 2cm-wide strips (you should get 12). Then all you need to do is twist each strip about 4 or 5 times (see picture on page 57). They are now ready to freeze if you wish, or you can cook them straight away. Place the twists together on a baking tray, grate over some **Parmesan cheese,** and bake at 220°C/425°F/gas 7 for about 8 to 10 minutes, or until golden and crisp.

CALORIES	FAT	SAT FAT	PROTEIN	CARBS	SUGAR	SALT	FIBRE
171kcal	11.8g	5.8g	3.2g	14.1g	0.7g	0.4g	1.2g

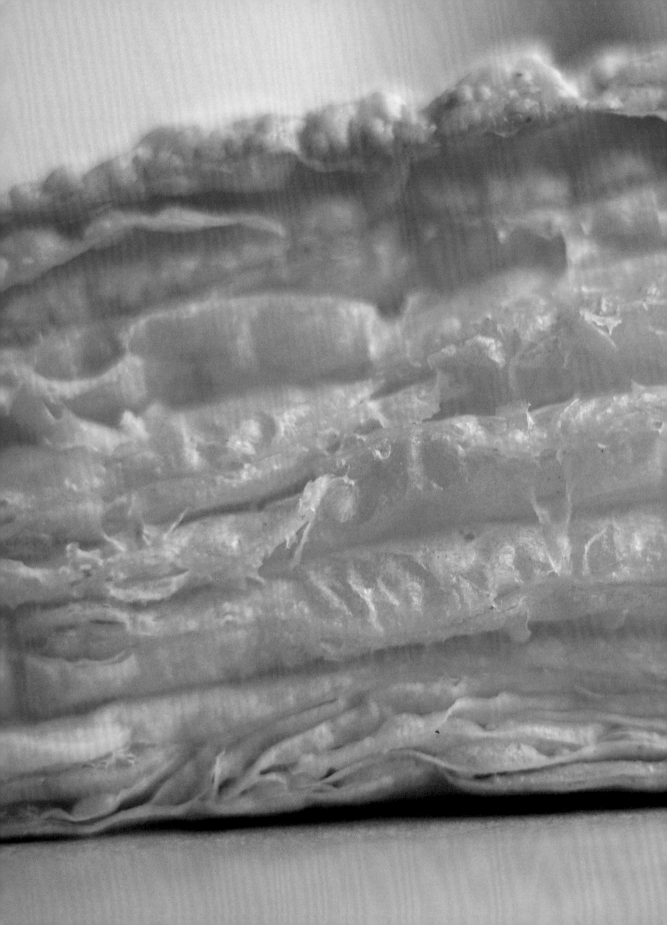

Quick Jammy Apple Tart On a floured surface, roll out the **puff pastry** to until just under ½cm thick. Get an 18cm plate and use this as a template to cut out 8 circles. Peel some **apples or pears,** quarter them, remove the cores and finely slice into slivers. Toss in a bowl straight away with just enough **sugar** to lightly coat the fruit, and a couple of tablespoons of freshly squeezed **orange juice.** Put 1 tablespoon of **jam** into the middle of each circle of puff pastry, and fan out the fruit slices on top. Fold in the sides to hold it all together, sprinkle over a little fresh **thyme,** and bake in the oven at 220°C/425°F/gas 7, or until the fruit has softened and the pastry is golden and crisp. Serve with crème fraîche or ice cream. Again, if you want to freeze these (uncooked) as last-minute lifesavers, then feel free to. You can cook them straight from frozen (at the same temperature), until the pastry is golden.

Mini Calzones with Prosciutto, Mozzarella & Tomato
Roll the **puff pastry** out into 8 x 18cm circles, as above. On one half of each circle lay a slice of **prosciutto,** followed by a squash-ball-sized piece of **mozzarella cheese.** Squash 1 ripe **cherry tomato** on top, add a few fresh **basil leaves,** and season with **sea salt and black pepper.** Wrap the prosciutto around the filling to hold it together, then **eggwash** the edges of the pastry and fold it in half, almost like a Cornish pasty. Pinch or crimp the sides together to seal the filling inside, and bake at 220°C/425°F/gas 7 until golden and crisp.

Sausage Rolls Buy some quality **sausages** – Cumberland ones are great – rip them open and discard the skins. Put the meat into a bowl and add a handful of roughly chopped **fresh herbs** (try rosemary, sage, thyme), then add one or two of the following: **orange or lemon zest,** some **chestnuts,** a little chopped **apple or pear,** and mix everything together to give you fantastically flavoured sausage meat. Roll out the **puff pastry** so it's 20cm wide and just under ½cm thick, dusting with **plain flour** as needed. Cut the sheet of pastry in half, so you have two 10cm wide strips. Now get the sausage stuffing and divide it in half. Roll each half into a sausage shape and lay these along the length of the two pastry strips. **Eggwash** the pastry, roll it up, and then use the back of a fork to mark and seal the pastry so it's tightly wrapped up. Eggwash the top of each, and cut the roll into shorter pieces, if you want. Bake at 220°C/425°F/gas 7 until golden, crisp and puffed up. You can freeze the rolls uncooked – simply remove them from the freezer when you need them and cook them from frozen (at the same temperature), until golden and crisp. Nice with some pickle, a lump of Cheddar and a rocket salad.

5-Minute Wonders

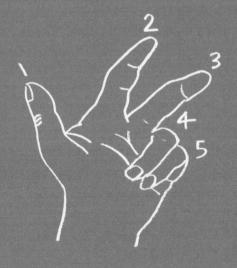

Just about everyone I know, including myself, comes home late and knackered quite a few times during the week. Did you know that 15 years ago the average time spent making a meal for the family was an hour – nowadays it's a measly 13 minutes! (And that's probably waiting for the microwave to go 'ding' while making a cup of tea.)

So I got to thinking that anyone making a quick dash round the supermarket on their way home from work could probably do with getting a little inspiration for dishes for one that can be made quickly when they get through the door. Bearing this in mind, the recipes here all use ingredients that you can pick up from any market or supermarket. I then decided to time myself making each of these dishes, which was fun! I tried to work reasonably slowly to give a realistic prep and cooking time. The results are pretty cool, especially considering that for some of the recipes, the time from the pan going on the heat to serving the food at the table was only 3 minutes! (My timing – you might need 5 to 10 minutes!) And nothing was compromised – all the dishes smelt great and tasted lovely. Each recipe has the time it took for me to make it – you never know, you might be able to beat me on some of them!

So if you're the kind of person who thinks they haven't got time to cook, or you run out of time (like we all do sometimes), then this chapter should be quite helpful to you. You know the thing: you're rushing around, you're busy, work seems to get later and later and on the way home you speed through the basket checkout, having picked up a chicken breast or some salmon and a selection of vegetables.

If you don't really find cooking all that relaxing, I hope these recipes will be fun, make you feel good and give you a nice dinner. It just goes to show you don't need hours to come up with some magic-tasting food.

A last note ... all the recipes in this chapter use pan-frying as the main method of cooking – I love this method, as it's totally immediate. But what you will need to get hold of is a large, non-stick pan – that will make your life even easier!

SALMON & COUSCOUS (5M 48S)

SERVES 1 • 75g couscous • 1 x 120g salmon fillet, skin on, scaled and pin-boned • olive oil • 1 small courgette, sliced into batons • 1 small handful of asparagus tips • 1 fresh red chilli, deseeded and finely chopped • 2 ripe tomatoes, roughly chopped • ½ a lemon • extra virgin olive oil • ½ a bunch of fresh coriander, leaves picked and roughly chopped • 1 tablespoon natural yoghurt

Put the couscous in a bowl, then just cover with boiling water. Pop a plate on top and leave to fluff up. Slice the salmon widthways into finger-sized strips, drizzle with olive oil, and season with sea salt and black pepper. Place the salmon strips into a small non-stick frying pan on their side, scatter over the courgette, asparagus tips and chilli, then cook for 2 minutes, turning the salmon halfway. Mix the tomatoes, lemon juice, 4 tablespoons of extra virgin olive oil and the coriander into the couscous and season to taste. Remove the salmon to a plate and add the couscous to the veggies left in the pan. Mix together, then put the salmon strips back into the pan on top of the couscous. Cover with a lid on and put back on a high heat for 1 minute. To serve, slide everything on to a plate and spoon over some yoghurt. Quick and tasty!

CALORIES	FAT	SAT FAT	PROTEIN	CARBS	SUGAR	SALT	FIBRE
456kcal	33.5g	5.7g	29.5g	9.7g	9.6g	1.2g	3.1g

HOT TUNA SALAD (4M 5S)

SERVES 1 • 1 x 200g tuna steak, ideally 2cm thick • olive oil • 1 handful of chunky bread, torn • 3 ripe tomatoes, quartered • ½ a bunch of fresh basil, leaves picked • extra virgin olive oil • ½ a lemon • 2 tablespoons natural yoghurt

Get a frying pan very hot. Rub the tuna with a little olive oil, season with sea salt and black pepper and sear for about 1 minute on each side (this will cook it rare). Crisp the bread until golden at the same time. Mix the tomatoes, crispy bread and 10 basil leaves in a bowl and stir in a little extra virgin olive oil and half the lemon juice. Season and put on a plate. Pound the remaining basil in a pestle and mortar and mix with the yoghurt. Season with salt, pepper and lemon juice. Place the tuna beside the salad and spoon over the sauce.

CALORIES	FAT	SAT FAT	PROTEIN	CARBS	SUGAR	SALT	FIBRE
400kcal	7.3g	1.9g	60.6g	24.9g	10.7g	1.6g	3.7g

PARMESAN FISH FILLETS
WITH AVOCADO & CRESS SALAD (4M 58S)

SERVES 1 • 2 tablespoons plain flour • 150g white fish fillets, skin off, pin-boned • 1 large egg, beaten • 50g freshly grated Parmesan cheese • olive oil • ½ a fresh red chilli, deseeded and finely chopped • ½ a ripe avocado, peeled, destoned and sliced lengthways • 1 punnet of cress • extra virgin olive oil • ½ a lemon

Get a frying pan really hot. Season the flour with sea salt and black pepper. Dust the fish fillets with the seasoned flour, then dip into the egg and press into the grated Parmesan, making sure the fish is nicely covered. Drizzle a little olive oil into the hot pan, and fry the fish fillets for a couple of minutes on each side until golden brown. Throw in the chilli. Mix together the avocado and cress with the extra virgin olive oil and lemon juice, and put on your plate with your fish fillets.

CALORIES	FAT	SAT FAT	PROTEIN	CARBS	SUGAR	SALT	FIBRE
779kcal	48.9g	16.1g	60.3g	26.5g	1.6g	2.4g	1.5g

CHORIZO & TOMATO OMELETTE (4M 58S)

SERVES 1 • olive oil • 30g Spanish chorizo sausage, sliced thickly • 1 ripe tomato, deseeded and sliced • 2 sprigs of fresh marjoram or flat-leaf parsley, leaves picked and roughly chopped • 3 large eggs • ½ a fresh red chilli, sliced • 1 spring onion, trimmed and finely sliced

Heat a little oil in a small frying pan, then add the chorizo and fry for 1 minute before adding the tomato and the marjoram or parsley. Whisk the eggs in a small bowl, add the chilli, season with sea salt and black pepper, and pour into the pan with the chorizo and tomato. Using a fork, mix the eggs around a little, then throw in the spring onion. Continue to cook until the eggs are nicely set, giving you a lovely little omelette. Great served with some dressed rocket.

CALORIES	FAT	SAT FAT	PROTEIN	CARBS	SUGAR	SALT	FIBRE
393kcal	28.9g	8.5g	29.8g	4g	3.5g	2.7g	1.4g

GINGERED CHICKEN WITH NOODLES (4M 41S)

SERVES 1 • 75g egg noodles • olive oil • 1 chicken breast, skin off, cut into 2.5cm strips • 5cm piece of ginger, peeled and thinly sliced • 1 fresh red chilli, deseeded and finely sliced • 1 teaspoon Chinese five-spice • 3 spring onions, trimmed and finely sliced • 1 dash of low-salt soy sauce • 1 tablespoon runny honey • ½ a bunch of fresh coriander, leaves picked and roughly chopped • ½ a lemon

Cook the noodles in a pan of boiling salted water according to the packet instructions. While the noodles are cooking, get a frying pan very hot, pour in 2 tablespoons of oil and let it heat through. Add the chicken strips, ginger and chilli. Toss together, then add the five-spice. Once the chicken is browned, add the spring onions, soy sauce and honey. Drain and add the noodles to the chicken with the coriander. Season to taste with sea salt and black pepper and serve immediately with a squeeze of lemon juice, to taste.

CALORIES	FAT	SAT FAT	PROTEIN	CARBS	SUGAR	SALT	FIBRE
701kcal	30g	4.5g	39.9g	73.7g	19.5g	2g	0.6g

BEEF WITH PAK CHOI, MUSHROOMS & NOODLES (5M 12S)

SERVES 1 • 75g thin rice noodles • 100g sirloin steak • olive oil • 1 teaspoon ground cumin • ½ a red onion, peeled and finely sliced • 1 thumb-sized piece of ginger, peeled and finely sliced • 1 fresh red chilli, deseeded and finely sliced • 1 small handful of shiitake and oyster mushrooms, brushed clean and torn up • 200ml quality chicken stock • 1 pak choi, quartered

Soak the noodles in the boiling water according to the packet instructions. Meanwhile, rub the beef with oil, sprinkle with the cumin and a pinch of sea salt and rub all over. Get a frying pan very hot and sear the beef on all sides. Add the onion, ginger and chilli, cook for a couple of minutes, then add the mushrooms, stock and pak choi. Drain and add the noodles to the pan. Stir well and correct the seasoning. Serve the noodles and pak choi in a big bowl, slice up the beef and place on top, then pour over the broth from the pan.

CALORIES	FAT	SAT FAT	PROTEIN	CARBS	SUGAR	SALT	FIBRE
600kcal	18.3g	6.5g	34g	73.1g	9.3g	1.5g	3.6g

PAPRIKA SIRLOIN STEAK WRAP (5M 45S)

SERVES 1 • 1 x 150g sirloin steak, fat removed • olive oil • 1 teaspoon smoked paprika • 1 handful of rocket • 2 ripe tomatoes, roughly chopped • 1 lemon • extra virgin olive oil • 2 tortilla wraps • 1 punnet of cress • 2 tablespoons houmous • 1 tablespoon soured cream

Get a griddle pan or frying pan very hot. Meanwhile, score each side of the steak and rub with oil. Sprinkle over the smoked paprika and season with sea salt and black pepper. Place on the griddle and cook for about 2 to 3 minutes on each side, depending on how thick the steak is and how you like it cooked. Mix the rocket with the tomatoes, and dress with lemon juice and extra virgin olive oil. Wipe the pan clean with a ball of kitchen paper, then heat the tortilla wraps on both sides, but don't let them go crispy. Slice up the steak and serve it on the tortillas with the salad, cress, houmous, soured cream and an extra pinch of paprika, if you like.

CALORIES	FAT	SAT FAT	PROTEIN	CARBS	SUGAR	SALT	FIBRE
762kcal	34.3g	8.8g	40.7g	79.4g	9.4g	3.7g	10.4g

SUPER-TASTY LAMB CUTLETS (4M 31S)

SERVES 1 • 75g couscous • 2 lamb cutlets, French-trimmed • 1 teaspoon ground cumin
• olive oil • ½ a red onion, finely sliced • 1 sprig of fresh thyme, leaves picked and
chopped • ¼ of a fresh red chilli, deseeded and finely chopped • 2 ripe tomatoes •
½ a bunch of fresh flat-leaf parsley • extra virgin olive oil • 1 lemon

Get a frying pan very hot. Put the couscous in a bowl, then just cover with boiling water. Pop a plate
on top and leave to fluff up. Flatten the cutlets with the palm of your hand, then dust on both sides
with sea salt, black pepper and cumin. Drizzle with a little olive oil, then place in the pan, turning
when browned on one side. Add the onion, thyme and chilli and move the ingredients around so
they cook evenly for the next couple of minutes. Finely chop the tomatoes and most of the parsley
and mix into the couscous with a good lug of extra virgin olive oil and a squeeze of lemon juice.
Season to taste. Serve the couscous with the lamb and onions on top, and sprinkle over the parsley.

CALORIES	FAT	SAT FAT	PROTEIN	CARBS	SUGAR	SALT	FIBRE
593kcal	25g	9.8g	27.1g	72.4g	12.9g	1.2g	7.3g

JAMIE'S LUNCHBOX

CIABATTA SANDWICH OF GRILLED VEGETABLES
WITH PESTO AND MOZZARELLA

SQUASHED FIG, BASIL AND PARMA HAM
SARNIE IN TOMATO BREAD

THE BEST PRAWN SANDWICH WITH BASIL
MAYONNAISE AND CRESS

THE BEST BEEF SANDWICH WITH CRUNCHY
LETTUCE, ENGLISH MUSTARD AND GHERKINS

SMOKED SALMON, LEMON AND CRÈME FRAÎCHE

CHEESY STEAK SANDWICH

DOUBLE-DECKER CHEDDAR CHEESE
SANDWICH WITH PICKLED ONION AND CRISPS

BANANA AND BLUEBERRY FRENCH TOAST

QUESADILLAS WITH GUACAMOLE

CRISPY PEKING DUCK IN PANCAKES

Sandwiches are the most widely eaten type of food in the UK, and probably in most western countries. Every country seems to have its own style of sandwich, from the croque monsieur in France to the hamburger in America, to the quesadilla in South America, to Peking duck pancakes in China. And of course there is the good old doner kebab from Turkey!

I feel quite strongly about this chapter, because even though lots of people turn their noses up when it comes to sandwiches or think they are cheap, nasty and naff, or even a bit of a joke in the culinary world, the truth is they don't have to be.

You might think there's nothing remotely exciting about sandwiches, but the fact is that you can make them in seconds, they're really portable and there's no excuse for them not to be damn tasty.

If you talk to your friends about their favourite sandwiches, you may agree on some, like a bacon sarnie for instance, but when you carry on talking you realize that actually you've all got your own way of making it. A discussion will no doubt follow, with remarks like, 'You want to toast the bread,' 'Gotta have brown sauce,' 'No, ketchup,' or that there's got to be melted cheese or a soft fried egg on top. In one particular conversation, with my friend John, things went downhill when he confessed that he has peanut butter, banana and bacon sandwiches and swears it's the best in the world – freak! But if he's happy with it, that's fine. Another old chef mate, Chris, likes a triple-decker with bacon, beetroot and lettuce. And my thing is that I like to cut my loaf lengthways, using just thick smoked bacon. I cook the bacon first on the griddle pan, then toast the bread in the pan juices to give a kind of fried bread vibe.

I think the reason some people aren't too keen on sandwiches is because they're often similar and can get boring, but there's no need to make or buy the same ones all the time. Here's a collection of the sandwiches that make me smile and make my tummy rumble when I think about them. Some make me want to be back on holiday, and others make me want to come home. I'll also give you some tips on how to turn a boring old lunchbox into a portable gourmet restaurant.

MY KINDA LUNCHBOX

- A really nice sarnie made with your favourite filling. Try using brown or wholemeal bread instead of white, and try not to stick to the same filling every day, if possible.

- Having a carton of unsweetened fruit juice can occasionally make a nice change from water – and it counts towards your daily fruit portions.

- Instead of the usual apple, which can become a bit boring, try a little bunch of grapes, half a melon, some sliced mango, half a papaya with a wedge of lime, or a kiwi, and include a spoon.

- Try and get your kids eating a little dried fruit – there is such a big choice now ...

- I believe that a little treat is fine from time to time if you've got a balanced lunch.

- If you want to embarrass your kids, leave a little note for them in their lunch – like my mum used to do with me!

- While your kids are young, make a little salad an everyday thing, not a 'healthy' thing that is only eaten occasionally.

SOME LUNCHBOX TIPS

DID YOU KNOW ...

• If you freeze a water bottle or carton of drink, it will make your lunchbox into a mini coolbox – both hygienic and great, because by lunchtime it will have melted, giving you a lovely slushy cold drink.

• It's so important to spread your butter evenly from corner to corner, to act as a waterproof layer – this will help to prevent soggy sandwiches!

• There are so many different types of bread available these days, so ditch your plain white or wholemeal every now and again and give these a go with different fillings: rosemary and raisin with cheese, ciabatta with mozzarella and prosciutto, sun-dried tomato bread with ham, or poppy-seed rolls with chicken.

• A little fruit eaten every day can only be a good thing – mix up the colours and varieties to maximize the vitamins and minerals you get. If you wrap your fruit in a napkin, you'll find that it won't get bruised.

• Kids can enjoy salads if they taste nice, if they're not soggy and if they're fun and a little interactive. So put a few slivers of Parmesan or some crumbled feta in a bag with a few cherry tomatoes and some nice mixed leaves. Make a separate wrap of dressing – 1 teaspoon of lemon juice with 2 of extra virgin olive oil wrapped in a little clingfilm. Kids can squash the tomatoes up in the bag, add the dressing and shake it up – they'll love it!

• Thermos flasks are great to use – you can buy small ones which are perfect for taking hot food with you like soup, meatballs or sausages in tomato sauce. The possibilities are endless ...

CIABATTA SANDWICH OF GRILLED VEGETABLES WITH PESTO & MOZZARELLA

This sandwich is good for using up grilled veg like asparagus, courgettes, fennel and aubergine – wonderful just grilled on a griddle pan and dressed with some extra virgin olive oil, a squeeze of lemon juice, sea salt, black pepper and fresh herbs. I keep any leftovers, stuff them into a chunk of ciabatta spread with 1 tablespoon of pesto (see page 34) and add a little torn-up mozzarella cheese. You could also add some grated Parmesan if you like. Slices of prosciutto or grilled chicken pieces go really well, too.

Wrap the sandwich up tightly in greaseproof paper and tin foil before putting it in your lunch box. Usually some juices come out of the mozzarella, so give the sarnie a good press down when you've finished making it to let the bread soak it all up and actually become more tasty because of it. When I eat this sandwich, I peel off the paper and foil from one side and keep peeling back as I eat – this way I don't get juice all over myself!

CALORIES	FAT	SAT FAT	PROTEIN	CARBS	SUGAR	SALT	FIBRE
414kcal	18.1g	5.5g	17g	49.2g	4.7g	2.3g	3.3g

SQUASHED FIG, BASIL & PARMA HAM SARNIE IN TOMATO BREAD

This filling is great with all kinds of bread. Here I've used it in some lovely tomato bread. Lightly butter the bread, tear open a beautifully ripe, sticky fig – generally when you think they are a little over-ripe and their skins have started to crack, they are perfect – and squash it into one side of the bread. Rip over some fresh basil, then lay over some Parma ham, and even some mozzarella cheese or shaved Parmesan if you like. This also works well toasted or Brevilled and it's best served fresh, with an Italian beer.

CALORIES	FAT	SAT FAT	PROTEIN	CARBS	SUGAR	SALT	FIBRE
178kcal	17.4g	9.8g	16.3g	40.9g	6.7g	1.8g	5g

THE BEST PRAWN SANDWICH
WITH BASIL MAYONNAISE & CRESS

Obviously this is best made with great cooked prawns and 1 tablespoon of homemade mayonnaise or aïoli. But I know that you may think, 'I can't be bothered to make my own.' Is it worth it? Yes, definitely. However, you will still get good results using jarred mayo (although homemade is much more of a treat) if you smash up ½ a bunch of fresh basil and mix it in. Add a squeeze of lemon juice, and sea salt, black pepper and cayenne, to taste. Toss the prawns in the basil mayo till they're well coated (you can chop some of them up if you like).

Get yourself two slices of decent white or brown bread and butter them well. Take a punnet of sandwich cress, which is nice and crunchy and peppery. Put half the cress on the bread, with the prawns on top, followed by the rest of the cress. Put the other slice of bread on top of that, squeeze down, and cut diagonally into four. Great served with a few plain crisps. And you know what? This sandwich is so good that it would even go down well with a glass of wine.

PS If you're going to have this sarnie in a packed lunch, make the sarnie up just before eating so it doesn't go soggy. To do this, lay some clingfilm out and dollop your prawn mixture in the middle, then gather the clingfilm up and tie it in a knot. When you're ready to make up your sandwich, pop the clingfilm open and squeeze the prawns and mayo out. What will the office say about that?!

CALORIES	FAT	SAT FAT	PROTEIN	CARBS	SUGAR	SALT	FIBRE
449kcal	25.7g	6.8g	19.1g	37.7g	3.6g	2.1g	4.4g

BAKERY

st john bread and wine, commercial street, london
amazing eccles cakes and bread

THE BEST ROAST BEEF SANDWICH WITH CRUNCHY LETTUCE, ENGLISH MUSTARD & GHERKINS

This sarnie is best made using a really fluffy loaf with a crispy crust. Butter two slices of bread well, then lay ragged slices of cold, rare roast beef – or use pastrami if you like – over one slice. Place a small handful of crunchy lettuce, such as Romaine or cos, over the top, then some thin slices of large sweet and sour gherkins. I like to spread the other slice really generously with strong English mustard, season well with sea salt and black pepper, then place it on top of the first slice. Delicious served with chips. (And if your eyes don't water, you need more mustard!)

CALORIES	FAT	SAT FAT	PROTEIN	CARBS	SUGAR	SALT	FIBRE
494kcal	16.7g	8.5g	41.4g	47.8g	3.8g	2.8g	3.3g

DOUBLE-DECKER CHEDDAR CHEESE SANDWICH WITH PICKLED ONIONS & CRISPS

By no means am I condoning this as a 'healthy' meal, but once in a blue moon I make this sandwich for myself. The texture and crunch of the crisps takes me straight back to being seven years old, when I used to make picnics for my mates Jimmy, Andy the gasman and Guy Allum. I have the good fortune of being able to visit two of the best cheese shops in England – Neal's Yard and La Fromagerie – both of which are a constant source of information and inspiration to me when it comes to new cheesemakers. Even though their advice, suggestions and knowledge are genius, I find it hard to resist my own addiction to something which would make their hair stand on end … a sandwich lightly buttered and layered with finely sliced pickled onions and the best Cheddar I can get my hands on, cut into 3mm slices. As I construct the layers, I put a few plain or salt and vinegar crisps in between the bread and, like popping those plastic air bubble things, I get rather too much pleasure from pushing down on the bread and hearing them crush. Give me a pint of Hoegaarden and in two minutes it's all over! I know for a fact that Patricia from La Fromagerie would say that the vinegar from the onions would kill the cheese and give you indigestion, but somehow I don't care! Sorry, Pat! xxx

CALORIES	FAT	SAT FAT	PROTEIN	CARBS	SUGAR	SALT	FIBRE
773kcal	39.1g	19.8g	26.6g	83.9g	4.6g	2.8g	5g

RETURN OF THE BREVILLE

The other day I was in Argos getting some bits and pieces when I saw this sandwich Breville in the shape of a cow, called Daisy. With my youngest daughter being called Daisy, and with writing this chapter, I thought I'd buy one. And it actually moos when I open it – I'm not kidding! Even though I'm not really a fan of kitchen gizmos, the actual end result from toasting a sandwich in a Breville is fantastic, as you have wonderfully crisp outsides but with a lovely oozy filling. They are also incredibly quick to use. I always get caught out, though, as toasted sandwiches can be dangerously hot inside. I always end up burning my tongue if I'm too hungry. Like pizzas, all Breville sandwiches are pretty damn good when eaten cold, too.

Things to bear in mind when making a good old Breville sarnie:

• Don't go too thick on the bread

• Square bread fits the best

• Lightly butter the bread on both sides, or use some olive oil, so it goes really golden and chewy

• Whatever combination you go for, a nice stringy cheese is essential and it's best to have it on the top and bottom pieces of bread with the other fillings in the middle

Just to get you thinking, here are some great combos:

- Leftover roast pork with Taleggio cheese. Dress a few fresh sage leaves with some olive oil and place on the outside of the bread before toasting – they will go crisp and taste fantastic

- Tacky but nice – ham with mustard or pineapple and Red Leicester cheese

- Cooked cold sausage sliced up with Cheddar cheese and Worcestershire sauce

- Tomato, mozzarella cheese and pesto (see page 34) – a good tip is to squeeze the tomato seeds out before slicing it up as this makes the sandwich less soggy

- One of the best indulgences is leftover meatballs with fresh basil and mozzarella cheese really squashed down. Heat the meatballs up first before using them

- Cheddar cheese and Stilton with red onion chutney

- Leftover mashed potato with sliced spring onions, Cheddar cheese and mustard

PS Even though my Breville is very cute and funny and it draws a lot of interest from my little kiddies, I don't think it's very wise to keep it out on the worktop as it gets so hot. Always remember to unplug it, make sure your kids can't reach it while it's cooling down, then pack it away (maybe I've turned into the worrying parent I thought I'd never be!).

SMOKED SALMON, LEMON & CRÈME FRAÎCHE SANDWICH

This is my favourite sarnie ever! Even from a very early age I knew it was something special. My family run a pub restaurant in the countryside, so we always had lovely smoked salmon. When I was about ten I used to play with the travellers who came to our village every summer to dig potatoes. One of them, Guy, used to have jam sandwiches every day, and one day I gave him one of my smoked salmon ones. I told him to squeeze on some lemon juice before he took a bite, and his face was just a picture! It was one of those defining moments that really inspired me to cook for ever. His taste buds were obviously saying, 'Wake up, this is Heaven!', and he loved it.

I am a firm believer in the simple smoked salmon sarnie: all you need is thinly sliced wholemeal or rye bread and cured wild salmon – an absolute joy. To make this perfect sarnie, lightly butter the bread, then get 1 tablespoon of crème fraîche and squeeze in the juice of half a lemon, with sea salt and plenty of black pepper, to taste. I like to place a layer of salmon on a piece of the bread, spreading over the lemony crème fraîche, then place the final layer of smoked salmon over the top with the other piece of brown bread. For an extra twang, you can sprinkle the salmon with very finely grated lemon zest. You can cut the crusts off and quarter the sandwich, but I just like to tuck into the whole thing. The crème fraîche really finishes it off and it explodes in your mouth. Lovely.

CALORIES	FAT	SAT FAT	PROTEIN	CARBS	SUGAR	SALT	FIBRE
396kcal	20.5g	10.6g	17.9g	37.6g	3g	3.1g	6.4g

SCOTTISH PETE'S CHEESY STEAK SANDWICH

My mate Peter Begg is one of my best friends and a fantastic cook. He used to work in the circus when he was younger, where he ran a kind of roulette stall, and this kept him busy for a few months travelling round America. Apart from some of his colourful stories about the bearded lady and the tattooed man, I remember the passionate way he talked about the cheesy steak sandwiches – apparently thousands of these would be sold from stalls in this travelling circus.

It basically involves getting a long submarine roll or baguette and heating it in the oven at 150°C/300°F/gas 2 for 5 minutes, or until it's just warmed through. Get yourself a nice piece of rib-eye, sirloin or rump steak – not too thick – and bash it out with your fist or a rolling pin to make it a little thinner and to tenderize it. Season with sea salt and black pepper and lay it on a very hot griddle pan. Obviously you can cook it to your liking, but I do mine medium-rare.

Once the steak is nicely seared on one side, turn it over and immediately grate Provolone cheese over the top so it melts from the heat of the steak and mixes with the juices. Once the other side is done, place it on a board, slice it up, and stuff it into the baguette or submarine roll with some wild rocket. Pour some of the steak juice over the bread, squeeze over some yellow American mustard and tuck in. Sliced onions also go really well with it, so if you have some, they can be cooked next to the steak in the pan.

CALORIES	FAT	SAT FAT	PROTEIN	CARBS	SUGAR	SALT	FIBRE
639kcal	16.9g	8.1g	48.3g	82.3g	4.6g	3.3g	5.7g

the father of these boys made sandwiches at this café in east london for 25 years. now they have taken over – respect and good luck!

BANANA & BLUEBERRY FRENCH TOAST

This is the kind of sandwich that can be eaten for breakfast on special occasions or even for dessert. Feel free to vary the fruit that you use – my missus likes strawberries and bananas, while my daughter Poppy likes banana with blackberries and blueberries.

All you do is get two slices of nice medium-cut white bread and lightly butter them on both sides. Toss the fruit combination in a little runny honey or sugar just to sweeten it a bit. A little mashed banana holds it all together quite nicely.

Beat a couple of eggs up in a bowl with 1 tablespoon of caster sugar, then dip both slices of bread in the sweet egg mixture so it's egged on both sides. Let the excess drip off then spread the fruit mixture on one slice, leaving a slight space around the edges of the bread. Put the other slice on top and press down – the egg will help the fruit to stick. Fry in a little unsalted butter in a medium hot pan on both sides, pushing down so that the fruit is pressed into the bread. Once the bread is golden and slightly crisp, dust with icing sugar and serve with a dollop of yoghurt, crème fraîche, cream or ice cream, with any remaining fruit mixture spooned over.

CALORIES	FAT	SAT FAT	PROTEIN	CARBS	SUGAR	SALT	FIBRE
549kcal	20.9g	11g	15.5g	79g	41g	1.1g	3.5g

QUESADILLAS WITH GUACAMOLE

A quesadilla is basically a Mexican-style stuffed pancake, like a toasted sandwich, made with two tortillas sandwiched together with a cheese-based filling. They are warmed through and served with guacamole and soured cream and are one of my favourite things to eat – Jools and I tend to have them every Saturday because we love them so much!

To make the guacamole I use 2 or 3 ripe avocados, 2 or 3 ripe deseeded tomatoes and a couple of deseeded red chillies, and I throw all this into a food processor with a handful of peeled and chopped spring onions and a good handful of fresh coriander. Once this has been chopped up nice and fine, I add a couple more chopped tomatoes, a good pinch of sea salt and half of another avocado, chopped, to give it a nice chunky texture. Transfer everything to a bowl and season carefully with salt, black pepper and a good squeeze of lemon or lime juice. If you decide to buy ready-made guacamole, which is a bit lazy but probably very realistic, you can put it into a bowl and chirp it up a bit with a squeeze of lemon juice and a bit of chilli to give it a kick.

To fill the quesadillas you will need a couple of big handfuls of grated Cheddar and/or Red Leicester cheese, some finely sliced spring onions, a couple of handfuls of chopped fresh coriander, and a red pepper and some red or green chillies, all deseeded and finely chopped. Mix all this up in a bowl and then sprinkle a handful between two layers of tortilla and press down. You can make up 4, 10 or even 20 quesadillas and keep them in the fridge until you need them if you want.

Some people like to fry them in oil, but this makes them greasy and is not all that healthy. You can grill them, but I like to put them in a dry non-stick frying pan on a medium heat, so that after about 1 minute and 30 seconds on each side you are left with a really crispy outside and an oozy, stringy filling. Serve the quesadillas cut into quarters, with the guacamole, soured cream and a beer.

PS You can also posh them up a bit using grilled chicken or seafood, leftover pork, shellfish, or a selection of grilled vegetables.

CALORIES	FAT	SAT FAT	PROTEIN	CARBS	SUGAR	SALT	FIBRE
327kcal	13.8g	4.8g	10.1g	43.4g	5.3g	1.6g	4.1g

THESE VALUES ARE BASED ON ONE QUESADILLA

CRISPY PEKING DUCK IN PANCAKES

SERVES 6

Peking duck is something that has always been very close to the Oliver family. Bizarrely enough, the fact that my parents ran a pub restaurant meant that we very rarely went out for dinner as a family, but when we did, my old man used to take us out to this Chinese restaurant in Sawbridgeworth where we all fell in love with Peking duck.

You probably don't think of Peking duck pancakes as sandwiches, but they really are. Everyone has their own little thing about it – Jools loves the plum sauce; I love the crispy duck skin; and my Grandad, bless his cotton socks, could not use chopsticks and thought he'd never get fed, because I would spin the round table in the middle to make sure I got the prime piece of duck before anyone else. There are hundreds of ways of cooking duck in Asian cultures – steamed, roasted, pumped up with bicycle pumps to remove the meat from the skin – but we're at home and so we can't do with all this mucking about. My way is simple and it works ...

Preheat the oven to 180°C/350°F/gas 4. Rub a 2kg duck with sea salt, inside and out. Dust the bird all over with Chinese five-spice and grate some ginger and rub it round the cavity, leaving the ginger inside to flavour. Place the duck in a roasting tray and put it into the oven, checking it every so often and spooning away the excess fat that has rendered out of the duck. Generally, after 2 hours it will be perfect – the leg meat will pull off the bone and the skin will be wonderfully crisp. You don't always need to, but I sometimes turn the heat up to 200°C/400°F/gas 6 for a short while until it's really crispy.

While this beautiful bird is cooking, make the plum sauce. Chuck 10 or 12 destoned plums into a pan with 5 tablespoons of sugar, a couple of pinches of five-spice, 2 tablespoons of low-salt soy sauce, ½ a teaspoon of chilli powder and a splash of water. Bring to the boil, then simmer until you get a nice shiny pulp. Remove the plum skins if you want to, but I usually leave them in. Sometimes I add a little grated orange zest, as this goes well with duck. Put the sauce to one side to cool before serving it, and taste to check the seasoning. As for the spring onions and cucumber, that's straightforward. Finely slice them. I strongly advise buying pre-made pancakes which you can place in a steamer or microwave and slowly steam until nice and hot. The bamboo steamers are only a few quid from Chinese supermarkets, so it's worth getting hold of some and they're great to serve at the table.

Once the duck has cooled a little bit, use two forks to shred up all the meat, discarding the bones. I remember the Chinese lady at the restaurant in Sawbridgeworth doing this. You can do the same, putting all the meat with its crispy skin on to a serving plate. Take a pancake, place some duck, a bit of spring onion, a little cucumber and a dollop of plum sauce on to it, then roll it up – lovely.

CALORIES	FAT	SAT FAT	PROTEIN	CARBS	SUGAR	SALT	FIBRE
587kcal	37.8g	10.8g	23.3g	40.1g	22.4g	1.2g	2.8g

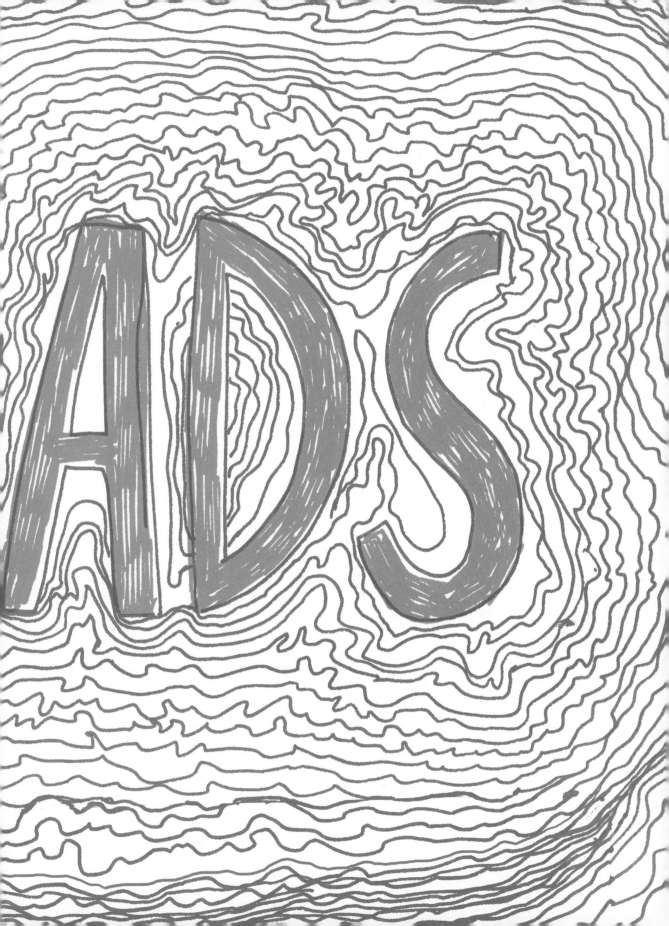

I'm really pleased with this chapter because I was thinking that I'd covered just about every great salad in my previous books, yet this year I've been completely inspired by salads from all over the world – India, Morocco, France, Japan, America – so I've included them here. Most of them are really simple and cheap to make, but they're some of the best salads I've ever had, whether served as a starter or as a side dish with something else. From the chop salad on page 111, which is really fun and quick to make, to really unusual things like the veggies with the mint and pea yoghurt on page 129, which involves everyone getting stuck in and looks totally different to any other salad you've ever seen.

I've used fresh horseradish in a few of the recipes as I have a real thing for it. It's a fantastic root that grows absolutely everywhere. I keep a spade in the back of my car at all times, just in case I come across a nice clump of wild horseradish! If you get a chance, go and dig some up. A horseradish root looks like a parsnip and once you cut into it you'll get the smell straight away – like English mustard.

To prepare horseradish, all you have to do is wash the root, peel it and grate it finely. Add as much or as little as you like, to any recipe, but its best friends are tomatoes, fish, beef and beetroot. Mixed with crème fraîche or double cream with some lemon juice and seasoning it's great with beef, used in a Bloody Mary it's genius, and grated over preserved meats like bresaola or prosciutto it's fantastic.

PS My salads have taken a turn of genius lately because I planted some herbs that I got from jekkasherbfarm.com ... I suggest that you do the same as they are superb!

MOROCCAN-STYLE BROAD BEAN SALAD
WITH YOGHURT & CRUNCHY BITS

This is a really great combination of flavours, colours and textures and, of course, is best made with fresh in-season broad beans. The smaller beans can be used as they are, but the mid to large ones, with tougher skin, will need to be peeled after cooking. Just pinch the skin between your nails and the bean will pop out – simple. I think my broad bean combo is pretty much perfect, but you can try it with fresh cannellini beans as well if you fancy a change.

SERVES 4

4 large handfuls of podded
   broad beans
2 lemons
extra virgin olive oil
1 bunch of fresh mint,
   leaves picked

1 small red onion, peeled and
   finely chopped
1 teaspoon cumin seeds, bashed
1 pinch of dried chilli
olive oil
2 handfuls of stale breadcrumbs
300ml natural yoghurt

First of all pod the beans. When I'm doing mine I round up friends and family to get the job done quicker. I also put the larger ones in one bowl and the smaller ones in another – they'll need different cooking times. Blanch the beans in unsalted boiling water for a couple of minutes, giving the large ones a bit longer (don't add salt, as this will toughen the skins). Drain them and lay them flat on a tray to cool down slightly – this salad always works best when the beans are eaten slightly warm. If you're making it in advance, though, you could always give them a quick flash in the microwave just before serving. Remove the skins from the larger beans if necessary. Place in a bowl and dress with the juice of 1 lemon and three times as much extra virgin olive oil. Season with sea salt and black pepper, to taste. Add a little more lemon juice, if needed – feel free to adjust to your taste. At this stage I like to finely slice half the mint and add it to the beans while they sit and marinate for a little while.

In a shallow pan, on a medium heat, fry the onion, cumin seeds and chilli in a little olive oil until softened, stirring regularly. As the onions start to colour, add the breadcrumbs and mix well. Continue to cook until the crumbs are golden and crisp, then season them to taste and set aside. To serve, divide the yoghurt between four plates or bowls. Give the broad beans a final toss, add the rest of the mint leaves, and divide between the plates on top of the yoghurt. Finally, sprinkle over the warm spiced crunchy bits.

Sometimes I like to finely grate some lemon zest over the top to give a little edge. Fantastic served with grilled chicken or as a tapas or antipasti style thing. Also great with flatbreads, like pitta.

CALORIES	FAT	SAT FAT	PROTEIN	CARBS	SUGAR	SALT	FIBRE
290kcal	24.3g	5g	6.2g	12.6g	6.7g	0.7g	2.2g

MY FAVOURITE AMERICAN CHOP SALAD

I've had this salad loads of times in the States – the best place to try it. Especially in really cool, quaint 1930s-style diners, or what are called 'chop houses'. You can order not only a salad but a 'chop steak' as well. This is kind of like a burger but the meat is cut a lot coarser and is then pressed back into a steak shape, as opposed to a burger. It's served with fries and salad.

I've asked many people in diners why it's called chop salad and the only conclusion we could come to is that they chop all the ingredients up, which is fair enough! I've had fantastic ones and I've had really bad ones. The only defining point between the two is the combination of ingredients and the fact that the good ones are not wilted, but nice and fresh. It should be eaten immediately after it has been chopped and dressed. It shows that you can make everyday ingredients seem a bit special, and the picture even makes it look a bit posh! You'll notice that I dress it at the same time as making it, which I think is the best way of doing it.

Just think about it: instead of having a dinner party where you bring out six plates of salad, one for each place mat – a bit boring – you can add a bit of theatre by bringing out a chopping board with a mezzaluna (rounded chopping knife), along with eight or nine individual whole ingredients. Start chopping these up and everyone will be wondering what's going on. And then you serve it and it will be fantastic. As well as being cool, it takes away the stress of trying to plate it up all prettily.

SERVES 6

1 red pepper, halved
1 fresh red chilli, halved
1 red onion, peeled
5 or 6 ripe tomatoes
½ a cucumber
200g feta cheese
2 Romaine or cos lettuces, or
   4 little gem lettuces

1 radicchio
2 bunches of mixed fresh herbs,
   such as flat-leaf parsley, basil,
   chives, mint
2 teaspoons English mustard
3 tablespoons white wine vinegar
extra virgin olive oil

Deseed the pepper and chilli. Get a large chopping board and either a mezzaluna (a double-handed rounded knife) or a chef's knife, and get ready to chop! It is important to chop the onion and chilli finely and to dice the tomatoes, pepper, cucumber and feta into 1cm pieces, as this will help to bind with the dressing when you come to mix it in. With the lettuce, radicchio and herbs, just make sure you chop them all into 1cm strips.

Make a well in the centre of the ingredients on your board. Add the mustard and stir it in with a teaspoon while you add the vinegar and 8 tablespoons of oil. Keep tasting to balance the flavours, and remember some vinegars can be harsher than others – just add a little more or less, to taste. Season well, taste, then add a tiny bit more seasoning, if needed, before bringing all the salad into the centre of the board. Mix it up and serve. Great with steak, fish or burgers.

CALORIES	FAT	SAT FAT	PROTEIN	CARBS	SUGAR	SALT	FIBRE
271kcal	23.2g	6.9g	7.6g	7.9g	7.2g	1.3g	3.4g

CRUNCHY KERALAN SALAD

This is a fantastic and really unusual salad that was inspired by a friend of mine called Das who runs the most terrific Indian restaurants in London, called Rasa. Although I have called it 'Keralan', it isn't really a true salad from there as you'd never find cress in Kerala! In Rasa, Das uses a lot of fresh coconut – which really is one of the most incredible flavours for making dishes like curries, or mixed into rice, breads, desserts and salads. You can now buy coconuts from most supermarkets, but if you can't find one, feel free to make this salad without it – it will still be pretty good but it won't have that special edge to it. Only make this when the mangos are silky smooth and not at all stringy. You should be able to cut through them like butter.

SERVES 6

1 small coconut (125g)
2 red peppers
4 punnets of cress
1 bunch of spring onions
2 ripe mangos, peeled

DRESSING
5cm piece of ginger, peeled
3–4 limes
extra virgin olive oil

First of all you need to crack open the coconut shell. I normally do this by placing it on a tea towel on a hard surface and giving it a wallop with a rolling pin or hammer. Once you've cracked it open, you can pull it apart (being careful not to spill the milk everywhere!), discarding the hard outer shell. The dark skin on the outside of the coconut's flesh doesn't bother me, especially if I'm grating it. But if you want to remove it, a speed-peeler works quite well.

Once you've got into the coconut, cut the peppers into quarters, remove the stalks and seeds, then finely slice. Trim the cress directly from its punnet (the easiest way to do this is to take the cress out of the punnet, slice the stalk-end off and discard it). Trim and finely slice the spring onions. Cut the mango flesh off the stones and finely slice it (there is a knack to doing this properly – if you look at the shape of the mango, the flat stone always lies the same way, parallel with the flattest sides, so you should be able to slice the flesh off with not too much wastage). Finely grate the pieces of coconut. Put all these ingredients into a large salad bowl.

Lime and ginger work together really well in the dressing. Finely grate the ginger and lime zest into a small bowl, then add the lime juice and 7 to 8 tablespoons of oil. Season to taste with sea salt and black pepper, and add more oil as necessary to balance the flavours of the dressing. Limes can be different strengths depending on their juiciness and size.

Dress the salad just before serving, saving any extra dressing for another day, and eat straight away. Great just as it is, or with some grilled prawns or satay chicken. Also lovely as a snack inside a wrap or flatbread. So even though the coconut may be a pain to prepare it's well worth it ...

CALORIES	FAT	SAT FAT	PROTEIN	CARBS	SUGAR	SALT	FIBRE
239kcal	21.7g	8.6g	1.9g	9.7g	9.4g	0.4g	2.4g

me and the lovely anne at kidbrooke school – week 2 … scary times!

SUMMER TOMATO & HORSERADISH SALAD

For this salad it's great to try and get a whole mixture of different tomatoes, at room temperature, nice and ripe. Let them sunbathe on the window ledge if need be! Try and get hold of fresh horseradish – give your greengrocer a challenge to get some in.

SERVES 6
4 large handfuls of mixed ripe tomatoes
extra virgin olive oil
red wine vinegar
½ a clove of garlic, peeled and grated
2 teaspoons fresh horseradish, finely grated, or jarred horseradish
½ a bunch of fresh flat-leaf parsley, leaves picked and finely sliced

Cut the bigger tomatoes into 1cm-thick slices. You can halve the cherry tomatoes or leave them whole. Sprinkle them all with a good dusting of sea salt, then put them in a colander and leave them for 30 minutes – the salt will draw the excess moisture out of the tomatoes, intensifying their flavour. Don't worry about the salad being too salty, as a lot of the salt drips away.

Place the tomatoes in a large bowl and dress with enough extra virgin olive oil to loosen (approximately 6 tablespoons), and 1 to 2 tablespoons of vinegar, but do add these to your own taste. Toss around and check for seasoning – you may or may not need salt, but will certainly need black pepper. Add the garlic. Now start to add the horseradish. Stir in a couple of teaspoons to begin with, toss around and taste. If you like it a bit hotter, add a touch more horseradish. All I do now is get some finely sliced flat-leaf parsley and mix this into the tomatoes. Toss together and serve as a wonderful salad, making sure you mop up all the juices with some nice squashy bread.

This salad is fantastic with roast beef, goat's cheese or jacket potatoes. And if you roasted these tomatoes in a tray with some sausages scattered around them, it would be nice.

CALORIES	FAT	SAT FAT	PROTEIN	CARBS	SUGAR	SALT	FIBRE
119kcal	12.1g	1.8g	0.6g	2.1g	2g	0.4g	0.8g

SMOKED TROUT, HORSERADISH & NEW POTATO SALAD

I'm pretty sure that smoked fish and new potatoes are a match made in heaven, but there are a few extras that can turn it into something even more memorable and comforting. A squeeze of lemon juice is one example, but horseradish is even better! Of course you can use the jarred stuff, which you can get creamed or preserved, but remember that you'll probably have driven past a hundred jars of the stuff growing wild, on the way to the market!

SERVES 4
800g new potatoes, scrubbed
4 tablespoons crème fraîche or soured cream
2 lemons
extra virgin olive oil
4 heaped teaspoons fresh horseradish, or jarred horseradish
1 bunch of fresh flat-leaf parsley
½ a bunch of fresh chives
1 small bunch of spring onions, trimmed and finely sliced
300g hot-smoked trout

Cook the potatoes in boiling salted water until tender, then drain. While still warm, but cool enough to handle, either cut them in half or squash them into a large salad bowl. Add the crème fraîche, the zest and juice of 1 lemon and 4 tablespoons of oil. Toss around, then season to taste with sea salt and black pepper. Add or grate in the horseradish, tasting as you go, then finely chop the parsley and chives and throw these into the bowl. Add the spring onions, tear in the smoked trout, and mix together. Now it's very important to balance your salad with more seasoning and maybe an extra squeeze of lemon juice. You may even want to give it more of a kick by adding some extra horseradish. Personally, I love to add a lot of horseradish and make it really hot. Great served as a starter, salad or even dinner if you love it as much as I do.

PS It's nice to try lightly grilling the fish if you prefer to eat it warm.

CALORIES	FAT	SAT FAT	PROTEIN	CARBS	SUGAR	SALT	FIBRE
449kcal	25.9g	7g	22.3g	31.8g	3.9g	2.7g	4.4g

RAW BEETROOT SALAD

The other day I had a nice little roast in the oven – comfort food for a great Sunday afternoon. I had a bunch of raw beetroot to use up, so I thought it would be good to have something nice and zingy to munch on while I was waiting for the chicken to cook – like some tapas or antipasti to get my taste buds going. You can get some great beetroots these days – fantastic colours.

I took the leaves off the beetroots, as I didn't need them for this salad (but it's worth remembering that they're edible and that they taste nicer than Swiss chard or spinach!). I washed the beets, then, using a speed-peeler, peeled them all into really thin slices and flavoured them with sea salt, black pepper, finely chopped fresh flat-leaf parsley and a little grated fresh horseradish to give a nice bit of heat. I left them for 5 to 10 minutes so that the acid from the horseradish would soften the beetroot. The horseradish is optional, but it gives a good twang.

This salad is lovely on a bit of toast, with maybe a splash of vodka or a little block of crumbled feta cheese. Really nice to pick at before you have dinner.

beautiful beetroots
picked fresh from
prince charles'
back garden
at highgrove.
can't be bad!

SUMMER CHICKPEA SALAD

Chickpeas are pretty under-used in this country, to be honest. In places like Morocco, Italy and Spain they are prized like our Jersey new potato. Still, we have a lot more choice now than we used to have. If you go to a Spanish deli or specialist counter, you will generally be able to find jars of cooked chickpeas in water and these are the ones you want to make this salad really good. They should look a little plumper than tinned chickpeas but, of course, both tinned ones or dried ones can be used successfully here, too.

This salad is a great one for making up as you go along; you can use different spices, sun-dried tomatoes and spicy chorizo sausages, for instance.

> SERVES 4
> 1 small red onion, peeled
> 1–2 fresh red chillies, deseeded
> 2 handfuls of ripe red or yellow tomatoes
> 1 lemon
> extra virgin olive oil
> 1 x 400g jar or tin of chickpeas, drained, or around 4 large
>   handfuls of soaked and cooked dried chickpeas
> ½ a bunch of fresh mint, chopped
> 1 bunch of fresh green or purple basil, leaves picked and torn
> 200g feta cheese

First of all, finely slice the red onion. Once that's done, finely slice the chillies then roughly chop the tomatoes, mixing them in with the onion and chillies. Scrape all of this, and the juice, into a bowl and dress with the juice of ½ a lemon and about twice as much oil. Season to taste with sea salt and black pepper. Heat the chickpeas in a pan, then add 90 per cent of them to the bowl. Mush up the remaining chickpeas and add these as well – they will give a nice creamy consistency. Allow to marinate for a little while, then serve at room temperature.

Just as you're ready to serve, give the salad a final dress with the fresh mint and basil. Taste one last time for seasoning – you may want to add the juice from the remaining lemon half at this point. Place on a nice serving dish and crumble over the feta cheese.

CALORIES	FAT	SAT FAT	PROTEIN	CARBS	SUGAR	SALT	FIBRE
173kcal	9.3g	4.1g	8.7g	13.8g	4g	1.2g	4.1g

there's nothing better than having a
simple picnic with your family

THAI WATERMELON SALAD

Watermelons are a lovely summery fruit but not all that useful as ingredients. However, you can sorbet them or fill them up with vodka, as I showed in my first book, *The Naked Chef*. And, bearing in mind that they are crunchy, watery and slightly sweet, they are fantastic in a salad with fish or even deep-fried squid. Or you could turn them into a snack, with some sea salt and crumbled feta cheese on top, as I have done here.

SERVES 4

¼ of a watermelon
1 big bunch of fresh coriander, leaves
   picked
2 handfuls of rocket
1 bunch of fresh mint, leaves picked
1 small bunch of radishes, finely sliced
1 handful of sunflower seeds
   or unsalted peanuts
100g feta cheese

DRESSING

5cm piece of ginger, peeled and
   finely grated
1 red, 1 yellow and 1 green chilli,
   deseeded and finely sliced
2 tablespoons low-salt soy sauce
6 tablespoons extra virgin olive oil
1 teaspoon sesame oil
3–4 limes

Remove the watermelon skin and cut the flesh into small cubes, removing as many seeds as you can be bothered to (but don't worry too much, as you can eat them and you'll hardly notice them).

When you pick the coriander leaves remove the stringier part of the stalks but keep the finer ones, as they are nice to eat. Place in a bowl with the rocket, mint leaves, watermelon and radishes. Put the ginger, chilli, soy sauce, extra virgin olive oil and sesame oil into a smaller bowl and add just enough lime juice to cut through the oil – the number of limes you use will depend on how juicy they are. Season to taste with sea salt and black pepper and make sure the dressing is well balanced.

Place the sunflower seeds or peanuts in the oven or in a pan and warm through, then roughly pound them up in a pestle and mortar or in a metal bowl using the end of a rolling pin. Dress the salad really quickly. (You can use more dressing if you wish, but any left over is great to keep in the fridge to use the next day.) Divide between the plates, sprinkle over the hot sunflower seeds or peanuts and crumble the feta cheese over the top.

CALORIES	FAT	SAT FAT	PROTEIN	CARBS	SUGAR	SALT	FIBRE
319kcal	27.9g	6.8g	7.5g	10g	8g	1.7g	0.5g

COOL CRUDITÉ VEGGIES
WITH A MINTED PEA & YOGHURT DIP

This dish is only as good as the vegetables you buy, so use that as your starting point and you'll be on to an absolute winner! Here are some tips on buying and preparing a selection of veg …

- In most supermarkets these days you can get fresh baby carrots with their green tops. Leave about 2.5cm of the tops on and just give the carrots a scrub.

- Do the same with some lovely radishes. You can get some marbled pink and white oval ones now, which are crunchy and peppery. Again, leave the tops on as these make good handles when it comes to dipping.

- Use nice crunchy lettuces. Sweeter lettuces like cos and Romaine are good for dipping – I try to use the inner part, keeping the outer leaves for another salad. I leave the stalk on and then cut the lettuce into quarters, and that way they stay in one piece, but you don't have to do this. The important thing is to get good chunks of vegetables. I like to contrast the sweet lettuces with slightly more bitter ones like radicchio or endive.

- If you've got some young asparagus that's just come into season, it's really nice eaten raw. Feel free to use your imagination on the veggie side. Little fingers of celery or celeriac are also good. However, you often come across people who use raw cauliflower with dips – I personally would prefer colonic irrigation! I think cauliflower and broccoli are just awful eaten raw, so I wouldn't suggest using them here.

> DIP
> 200g natural yoghurt
> 1 bunch of fresh mint, leaves picked
> 2 handfuls of fresh podded peas
> 1 handful of freshly grated Parmesan cheese
> ½ a lemon

Whiz the yoghurt and mint leaves in a food processor for 30 seconds or so. Add the peas and the Parmesan and whiz again – the peas will break down and the yoghurt will become green. Put into a bowl, correcting the seasoning with sea salt and black pepper and a good squeeze of lemon juice. When you add the lemon juice and peas to the yoghurt, quite often it splits and turns into a kind of cheese, but this is absolutely fine. It depends on the type of yoghurt you use and how acidic your lemon is. Just pour away any excess water. Usually, though, it doesn't split and is more like a purée, but both ways are good.

The best way to serve this is to put the dip into a bowl and have a big board next to it with the veggies on. It's a good sociable way to start a meal.

CALORIES	FAT	SAT FAT	PROTEIN	CARBS	SUGAR	SALT	FIBRE
86kcal	4.6g	2.9g	6.2g	5.2g	3.7g	0.7g	0.7g

JAPANESE-STYLE SATURDAY NIGHT STEAK

This idea comes from a fantastic restaurant called Ima-Ha-N in the Asakusa district of Tokyo where they poach thin slices of very tender beef in seaweed stock for just a few seconds before dipping them in a special sauce made from sesame seed paste, lime and soy – so delicious! The meat really melts in your mouth. British beef is great to use for this dish, although it's not quite as tender as Japanese beef. However, it does have loads more flavour, so I decided to invent a dish along the same lines that works best using our meat.

SERVES 2
2 x 150g sirloin steaks, ideally 2.5cm thick
½ a mooli (also known as daikon)
1 bunch of fresh crisp radishes
1 fresh red chilli
½ a bunch of fresh coriander, leaves picked
2 tablespoons tahini
1 teaspoon low-salt soy sauce
1 lime
olive oil

Take the steaks out of the fridge 15 minutes before you want to cook them. Put them on a plate and just leave to one side while you prepare the rest of the ingredients.

Peel the skin off the mooli, then continue to peel long strips off it and put these in a bowl. Slice the radishes into fine rounds, deseed the chilli and slice it thinly, and add both to the mooli strips. Tear in the coriander leaves. Add 2 tablespoons of water gradually to the tahini and mix until you have a smooth paste. Stir in the soy and most of the lime juice, then taste and add a little more lime, if needed. Mix until smooth.

Place a frying pan big enough to hold both the steaks at the same time without them touching on a high heat. Season the steaks well with sea salt and black pepper, rub them with a little oil, and place in the pan. Fry for about 8 minutes, turning every minute and lowering the heat to medium after the first minute. Rest the steaks for a couple of minutes before slicing them up thinly, tipping any juices from the steaks into the tahini sauce.

To serve, dress the salad with the sauce, mix in the slices of beef, and tuck in!

CALORIES	FAT	SAT FAT	PROTEIN	CARBS	SUGAR	SALT	FIBRE
413kcal	28g	8.6g	37.1g	3.3g	3.1g	1.4g	0.5g

CARROT & CORIANDER CRUNCH SALAD

I always think it's brilliant if you can turn the humble carrot into anything remotely cool or credible, especially in the salad world. You deserve to have a medal if you can come up with something amazing. If you're lucky enough to have vegetables in your garden, you'll know what I mean when I say freshness is everything. But those of you who haven't got a garden should buy the freshest-looking organic ones you can find.

I use a mandolin (use the guard!) to slice the carrots for this salad – it will give you long ribbony slices – but you can use a speed peeler, a coarse grater or do it by hand with a knife instead, if you prefer. As long as your results are nice and crunchy, that's all that matters.

This is really good as a starter, or try eating it with some little kebabs if you're having a barbecue, or stuffed into some pitta bread with sliced grilled chicken.

SERVES 4–6
6 medium carrots, peeled
1 big bunch of fresh coriander, leaves picked
4 teaspoons sesame seeds, toasted, or poppy seeds

DRESSING
1 orange
2 lemons
extra virgin olive oil
2 heaped tablespoons sesame seeds, toasted

First of all, slice the carrots or cut them up into fine ribbons, matchsticks or batons. Put them into a salad bowl with the coriander leaves and the sesame or poppy seeds. To make the dressing, finely grate the orange zest into a bowl. Squeeze in the orange juice, the juice of 1½ lemons and about four times the amount of oil. Lightly pound the toasted sesame seeds to a pulp in a pestle and mortar, then add to the dressing. Mix well, then season to taste with sea salt, black pepper and possibly more lemon juice to make it nice and zingy and you can taste it once you've dressed the salad. Once dressed, the flavour of the lemon will lessen, so get eating straight away.

CALORIES	FAT	SAT FAT	PROTEIN	CARBS	SUGAR	SALT	FIBRE
369kcal	34.5g	5.1g	2.2g	13.3g	12.5g	0.6g	4.1g

GOOD OLD FRENCH BEAN SALAD

I had this salad a while ago in a bistro in France and it was fantastic. You know, twangy and mustardy and so nice to eat as a starter before the main course arrived. It reminded me that sometimes cooking rules should be broken. We're told that beans should only be cooked until they're al dente, but I think we should cook them for a bit longer. I'd rather run my nails down a blackboard than eat a squeaky al dente green bean! So here's a recipe for properly cooked beans. Keep your eyes open for different coloured beans – green, yellow or black – as a mixture will make it even more interesting. And when preparing them, leave the wispy ends on as they look so nice.

SERVES 4
4 handfuls of French beans, stalk-ends removed
2–3 heaped teaspoons French mustard, to taste
2 tablespoons white wine vinegar
extra virgin olive oil
1 medium shallot, peeled and finely chopped
optional: 1 tablespoon baby capers
½ a clove of garlic, peeled and finely grated
optional: ½ a bunch of fresh chervil

Bring a pan of water to a fast boil, add the beans, put a lid on and cook for at least 4 to 5 minutes. Boiling the beans fast like this helps them to retain all their nutrients. Meanwhile, put the mustard and vinegar into a jam jar or bowl and, while stirring, add 7 tablespoons of oil to make a good hot French dressing. Season carefully with sea salt and black pepper, then add the finely chopped shallot, the capers (if using) and the garlic.

Remove one of the beans from the pan to check if it's cooked. If it holds its shape but is also soft to the bite, it's perfect. Drain in a colander. Now, while the beans are steaming hot, this is the perfect moment to dress them – a hot bean will take on more of the wonderful dressing than a cold one. It is best to serve the beans warm, not cold, and certainly not at fridge temperature because the flavours will be muted and boring. Serve the beans in a bowl, sprinkled with chervil (if using) – it's a delicate, crunchy herb that goes well with beans. Serve as a salad in its own right, or as an accompaniment to a main meal.

CALORIES	FAT	SAT FAT	PROTEIN	CARBS	SUGAR	SALT	FIBRE
215kcal	21.4g	3.1g	2.1g	3.6g	2.6g	0.8g	3.5g

SOUPS

You might think cooking soup is a simple option, but actually I've realized that it's a real treat and quite brave and cool to make it for a dinner party or your family. Not only that, but it's cheap and virtually foolproof, even for the most inexperienced cook! For the last six months I've had a soup on the menu at Fifteen every day and it always sells well.

All the soups in this chapter will provide a good canvas for you to understand how diverse and great soups can be. Like breads, they're almost culinary signposts in the way they can sum up the place that they're from. I can imagine outdoor workers or farmers in Britain on a miserable day tucking into a thick leek and potato or oxtail soup, the Frenchman with so many onions that he makes an event out of a French onion soup, the clever Italian mum using up all her leftover broken bits of pasta to finish off her minestrone. And then in places like Kerala in Southern India, where it's humid and hot, the heat of the chillies in their soups actually helps you to perspire and cool down. These soups say so much about people and their cultures.

I had a conversation with a taxi driver recently. This guy liked his food, he cooked a fair bit, but he was desperately concerned about his teenage daughter, who refused to eat fruit and vegetables. Her skin was bad, she was moody and unhappy, and he was worried about her. I think there are probably a lot of parents out there who feel like that about their kids. I would say it's mainly to do with kids' lack of interest about what goes on in the kitchen, so use this to your advantage. You can put some great veg into their food without them knowing about it. The taxi driver's daughter did happen to like freshly squeezed orange juice, so I suggested that he buy a juicer and then, if he was to put a tiny bit of carrot or raw beetroot through the machine and top it up with orange juice, he could get away with saying it was a blood orange drink. She also loved tomato soup, so he tried spiking her soup with other puréed veg and it worked. At the end of the day, I do think that honesty is the best policy, but if you need to be a bit sneaky, then things like fresh fruit juices, soups and stews are a wonderful way of using really wholesome ingredients that awkward eaters will unknowingly and gladly tuck into!

PUMPKIN RICE LAKSA SOUP

This is one of the best soups I've ever had. Laksa is a kind of brothy noodle stew, very often made with chicken and coconut milk. When I was coming up with the idea for this soup, I was thinking of the Anglo-Indian mulligatawny soup, which is made from rice, curry sauce and minced meat. If you're feeling a little bit theatrical, like I was, feel free to take the lid off the pumpkin, scoop out the flesh, and serve the soup in the pumpkin shell. Lovely!

PS If you have a food processor, you can put it to good use for this recipe! If you don't have one, then your pestle and mortar will come in handy instead.

SERVES 6

600g pumpkin, butternut squash, onion squash or acorn squash, halved, peeled and deseeded

1 small handful of lime leaves

2–3 fresh red chillies, deseeded and finely sliced

2 cloves of garlic, peeled and finely sliced

10cm piece of ginger, peeled

3 sticks of lemongrass, tough outer leaves removed

1 big bunch of fresh coriander, leaves picked, stalks chopped

1 heaped teaspoon Chinese five-spice

1 teaspoon ground cumin

olive oil

1 onion, peeled and finely sliced

550ml quality chicken or vegetable stock

200g basmati rice

2 x 400ml tins of light coconut milk

1–2 limes

optional: 1 fresh red chilli, sliced

optional: fresh coconut, finely grated

Chop the pumpkin or squash into 5cm pieces. To make the base of the soup, first chop, then whiz or bash up the following in your food processor or pestle and mortar until you have a pulpy mix: the lime leaves, chillies, garlic, ginger, lemongrass, coriander stalks, five-spice and cumin. Remove any stringy bits that remain in the pulp. Put this mixture into a high-sided pan with a little oil and the onion and cook gently for 10 minutes to release the flavours.

Add the pumpkin and the stock to the pan. Stir around, scraping all the goodness off the bottom of the pan. Bring to the boil, then reduce the heat and simmer with the lid on for 15 minutes, or until the pumpkin is soft. Add the rice and give it a really good stir – some of the pumpkin will start to mush up, but you'll also have some chunks. Continue to simmer with the lid on until the rice is cooked, then off comes the lid. Add the coconut milk, stir again, taste and season carefully with sea salt and black pepper. To give it a bit of sharpness squeeze in the lime juice – the amount will depend on how juicy your limes are, but the idea is to give the soup a little twang.

Serve the soup in warmed bowls or pour it back into the pumpkin shell. If you're going to do this, put the pumpkin shell into the oven to warm it through first. It's a great show-stopper for dinner parties. Finish sprinkled with the coriander leaves, or some sliced fresh chilli (if using), or grate over some fresh coconut if you have it, then tuck in.

CALORIES	FAT	SAT FAT	PROTEIN	CARBS	SUGAR	SALT	FIBRE
268kcal	10.6g	7.6g	6.1g	39.7g	7.7g	1.2g	3.5g

SCRUMPTIOUS SPANISH CHICKPEA & CHORIZO SOUP

I first tasted this soup when I was in Barcelona. It may not look like the prettiest dish – it actually looks quite frumpy – but the flavours are amazing. The smoky spicy chorizo and Spanish ham are lovely with the creamy texture of the chickpeas and spinach. Definitely give this a go. You will always get good results with this soup, but you'll come up with something really special if you can get hold of the best quality chickpeas, chorizo and ham. There's a little bit of chopping to do in this recipe, but you can use a food processor if you don't have much time.

SERVES 4

olive oil
100g chorizo sausage, finely chopped
1 onion, peeled and finely chopped
1 clove of garlic, peeled and finely chopped
2 sticks of celery, finely chopped
500g fresh spinach, chopped
8 ripe tomatoes, deseeded and roughly chopped

1 x 400g tin or jar of chickpeas, drained
1.2 litres quality chicken stock
50g pata negra, Spanish ham or prosciutto, finely chopped
extra virgin olive oil
2 large hard-boiled eggs

Put 2 tablespoons of olive oil into a large pan and add the chorizo. Allow to heat up and cook for 2 minutes, or until the fat comes out of the chorizo, then add the onion, garlic and celery. Turn the heat down and cook slowly for 15 minutes with a lid on and without colouring the onions. Now take the lid off – the smell and colour will be fantastic. Stir it around and get some colour happening now. Add the spinach, tomatoes, chickpeas and chicken stock. Bring to the boil, then lower the heat and simmer for around 40 minutes.

At this point you can remove about a third of the mixture and purée it in a blender or food processor. Pour it back into the pot, give it a good stir and season to taste with sea salt and black pepper. Remove from the heat and stir in the pata negra or ham and 2 or 3 tablespoons of good Spanish extra virgin olive oil. Divide between bowls and grate some hard-boiled egg on top. The egg was a bit unexpected when I was given this in Barcelona, but it actually adds a lovely richness to it.

CALORIES	FAT	SAT FAT	PROTEIN	CARBS	SUGAR	SALT	FIBRE
425kcal	27.5g	7.1g	22.8g	23.3g	12.7g	4.8g	9.6g

THE ULTIMATE ONION SOUP

The French often argue about where this soup originated – Lyon or Paris? Quite frankly I'd dispute whether it is actually from France and not Britain, as some of our onion soup recipes go back hundreds of years. However, most cultures and countries have a version of an onion-based or onion soup. In Italy there is a version called 'carabaccia' which is made from all different kinds of onion mixed together and slowly fried with chunks of potato and a little stick of cinnamon, which gives it the most incredible flavour. We only seem to get certain varieties of onion in our markets and supermarkets, but if you ever get down to a farmers' market, you'll see that they come in all different shapes and sizes.

SERVES 4

1kg onions, peeled and sliced
1 bunch of fresh thyme, leaves picked
6 cloves of garlic, peeled and
   finely sliced
1 fresh bay leaf
olive oil

1 good knob of unsalted butter
1.2 litres quality stock (beef,
   chicken or vegetable)
1 baguette or ciabatta
100g Gruyère, or other melting
   cheese

In a thick-bottomed non-stick pan, slowly fry all the onions with the thyme, garlic and bay in a good drizzle of olive oil and the butter. Cover with a lid and cook slowly for 15 minutes, without colouring, stirring occasionally so the onions don't catch on the bottom. The slower you cook them, the better. Remove the lid, turn up the heat and colour the onions until lightly golden. This will encourage a sweetness and a real depth of flavour. Add the stock, turn the heat down and simmer for 20 minutes. You can skim any fat off, but I think it adds good flavour.

Correct the seasoning with sea salt and black pepper. When it's perfect, pour into your serving bowls and place these on a baking tray. Now what I like to do, instead of slicing the bread all pretty and proper, is to tear it up. It's much more rustic and beautiful with all the knotty bits showing. Put the bread on top of the soup in each bowl, then drizzle over some olive oil and put the Gruyère on top. Place the baking tray in a preheated oven on a medium heat or under the grill (be careful not to crack your bowls or burn the bread) to lightly toast the bread and melt the cheese.

CALORIES	FAT	SAT FAT	PROTEIN	CARBS	SUGAR	SALT	FIBRE
357kcal	15.4g	7.9g	14.8g	43.5g	18.2g	4g	8.6g

THE REAL MUSHROOM SOUP

When I first moved to London I worked in the Neal Street Restaurant in Covent Garden. It was famous for its wild mushrooms, and my mate Gennaro used to go out every day during mushroom season to find them. It was in this restaurant that I tasted a real mushroom soup for the first time. Those awful tins of mushroom soup that we've all tasted just became a distant memory!

The nice thing about nearly all mushrooms is that, if cooked correctly, they do have wonderful flavour. If you were to use a field of Portabello mushrooms to make a soup, just adding a tiny bit of dried porcini into the base would make the whole thing more luxurious.

SERVES 6

1 small handful of dried porcini mushrooms
olive oil
600g mixed fresh wild mushrooms, such as chanterelles, girolles, trompettes de la mort, shiitake, oyster, sliced
2 cloves of garlic, peeled and finely sliced
1 red onion, peeled and finely chopped
1 bunch of fresh thyme, leaves picked
1 litre quality chicken or vegetable stock
1 bunch of fresh flat-leaf parsley, leaves picked and roughly chopped
1 tablespoon mascarpone cheese
1 lemon
optional: truffle oil

Place the porcini in a small bowl and just cover with boiling water and leave to rehydrate. Get a large casserole pan nice and hot, then add a good couple of lugs of olive oil and the fresh mushrooms. Stir around very quickly for 1 minute, then add the garlic, onion and thyme leaves and a small amount of sea salt and black pepper. After about 1 minute you'll probably notice the moisture cooking out of the mushrooms – at this point, add half the porcini, chopped up, and the rest left whole. Strain the soaking liquer to remove any grit, and add it to the pan. Carry on cooking for 20 minutes, or until most of the liquid disappears.

Season to taste, and add the stock. Bring to the boil and simmer for around 20 minutes. I usually remove half the soup from the pan and whiz it to a purée, then pour it back in, adding the parsley and mascarpone, and seasoning carefully, to taste.

You can serve this soup as you like, but there are a few things to remember when finishing it off. Mix together a pinch of salt and pepper with the zest of one lemon and the juice of half, then spoon a little of this into the middle of the soup. When you go to eat it, stir it in and it gives a wonderful flavour. Other things you can consider are little slices of grilled crostini put into the bottom of the bowls before the soup is poured over. Or you could even quickly fry some nice-looking mushrooms – like girolles, chanterelles or oysters – and sprinkle these on top of the soup. If I was going to use truffle oil, then I would use it on its own – a few drips on the top, just before serving.

CALORIES	FAT	SAT FAT	PROTEIN	CARBS	SUGAR	SALT	FIBRE
107kcal	8.8g	2.1g	3.7g	4.2g	2.6g	2.4g	1.6g

the mushroom man, tony booth, borough market – just look at the size of the morel in my hand!

SOUTHERN INDIAN RICE & SEAFOOD SOUP

This soup was first cooked for me by Das, my friend who runs the southern Indian restaurants in London called Rasa. I've based mine around his original recipe, and what's fantastic about it is that it's so easy to make. It only takes about 30 minutes, and the other great thing is that the ingredients are not particularly expensive, so it's economical. However, if you want to spend a little more and make it a bit luxurious using something like crab, then you can. The soup is just as good with frozen prawns and flaky white fish though. Use any selection of fish that you fancy – I like to use a good mixture of fresh-looking fish (John Dory, cod, haddock or red mullet all work well). Get it skinned and filleted, then all you have to do is chop it up. If you can find coconut oil, use a little of that, otherwise vegetable and sunflower oil are fine to use.

This really is one of my favourite soups – not too hot, but as you eat it you can pick out individual flavours. And there's something about having rice in a soup that makes it really scrumptious.

SERVES 4

5 tablespoons vegetable or
    sunflower oil
3 tablespoons brown
    mustard seeds
1 handful of fresh curry leaves
2 teaspoons cumin seeds
1 teaspoon garam masala
1½ teaspoons chilli powder
2 teaspoons ground turmeric
3 fresh red chillies, deseeded and
    finely sliced
10cm piece of ginger, peeled and
    finely grated

6 cloves of garlic, peeled and
    finely chopped
2 onions, peeled and finely chopped
2 handfuls of basmati rice
600g fish (see introduction), skin off,
    filleted and cut into 5–8cm chunks
1 x 400ml tin of light coconut milk
2 limes
1 bunch of fresh coriander, leaves
    picked and roughly chopped
optional: 3 tablespoons freshly
    grated coconut

Drizzle 5 tablespoons of oil into a large pan and place on a medium heat, then add the mustard seeds, curry leaves, cumin seeds, garam masala, chilli powder and turmeric. Cook for a few minutes and you'll get the most amazing smells filling the room from all these spices. Add the chillies, ginger, garlic and onions, then continue cooking gently until softened. Tip in the rice and 550ml water. Bring to the boil then reduce the heat and simmer gently for 15 minutes. Add the fish, the coconut milk and a tin's worth of water with a pinch of sea salt. Put the lid on the pan and simmer for a further 10 minutes, then stir well to break up the pieces of fish. Taste and correct the seasoning with salt and black pepper, then just before you serve it squeeze in the lime juice and stir in half the coriander. Serve in warmed bowls, sprinkle over some freshly grated coconut (if using) and rip over the rest of the coriander.

CALORIES	FAT	SAT FAT	PROTEIN	CARBS	SUGAR	SALT	FIBRE
493kcal	28.2g	8.4g	34.3g	29.9g	9.3g	1.1g	2.5g

skate and soup

FEEL-GOOD CHICKEN BROTH

When I was young and felt unwell with a cold or a headache, my mum would make this soup to help me feel better. It used to make me feel like a million dollars after I'd eaten it. It's probably one of the simplest soups to make because it just involves slowly boiling a whole chicken in a pot with a few roughly chopped root veg. The fat marbles on top during cooking, but underneath it is nice and clear, like a consommé. Like consommé, if you want to serve this at a dinner party or you want to vary its flavour, the actual soup will always stay the same but the garnish that you add can differ, from mushrooms to florets of cauliflower to julienned veg. Another nice thing you can do is add a splash of sherry or port just before serving to give it a little twang. All these things are great to try, but I just really like my mum's simple chicken broth. Her secret ingredient was a rasher of smoked bacon, and sometimes she'd add a few sprigs of rosemary for the last ten minutes.

SERVES 6
1 x 1.5kg whole chicken
2 carrots, peeled and roughly chopped
2 sticks of celery, roughly chopped
1 rasher of smoked streaky bacon
2–3 sprigs of fresh rosemary
1 handful of shiitake mushrooms
optional: 1 splash of sherry or port
extra virgin olive oil

Put the chicken, carrot, celery and bacon in a large pan, cover with water and bring to the boil. Turn the heat down and simmer slowly for 1 hour 15 minutes, skimming the white residue off the top every now and again. Add the rosemary sprigs, shiitake mushrooms and sherry (if using) for the last 10 minutes, then remove the chicken from the pan. It should be perfectly cooked, and will be great for salads or sandwiches or for tearing into slivers to put into the soup. Season the soup with sea salt and ladle it through a sieve into bowls, trying not to disrupt it too much as you want to keep it reasonably clear. Add the chicken slivers and a few mushrooms to each bowl and drizzle with a little extra virgin olive oil. The finished thing should be a kinda clear consommé.

CALORIES	FAT	SAT FAT	PROTEIN	CARBS	SUGAR	SALT	FIBRE
197kcal	8.5g	2.2g	27.1g	2g	0.3g	0.5g	0g

ABLES

" CEBOLLA
TOMATE
LECHUGAS
ZANAHORIA
Señora "

Veg

A lot of people turn their noses up at vegetables and I think it's because, in general, the British are known for just boiling the hell out of them – whether they're using root veg or greens – and it's incredibly boring. However, I think that in the last five years people have been getting more into veg, and what I really wanted to put across in this chapter is that, actually, a good veg dish can completely set off a dinner when served alongside some simply cooked fish or meat.

Having now experienced a few trips abroad to America and Australia, as well as tours all round Britain, there's one thing that I've come to realize and that is that a lot of posh restaurants and many great chefs have a real lack of good veg on their menus. This is such a shame – I think we should be proud to have vegetables on our plates.

Seasonality is incredibly important when it comes to eating the best vegetables available to us. A lot of brilliant chefs think it's OK to use asparagus or broad beans four months out of season. And I know that supermarkets are guilty of supplying vegetables for twelve months of the year. But if you learn how to shop for veg when they are in season, you will benefit hugely. It's not just about the nutritional and flavour benefits of seasonal produce, it will also save you loads of money! Farmers' markets are a great place to shop because the vegetables will probably have been harvested just hours before.

Experimenting with vegetables in cooking is easy, fun and a great confidence builder when it comes to creating your own ideas. The main principle of this chapter is to show you ways of cooking a selection of my favourite veg, along with some of their best friends in terms of flavour. A combo such as carrots, orange and rosemary or thyme pretty much always works well. Or take the turnip – a vegetable people turn their noses up at – which can be brilliant when pan-roasted with a swig of white wine and herb vinegar. Vegetable dishes like this can really make eating any rich meats like lamb, beef or venison a real joy.

TURNIPS

You can pretty much buy baby turnips all year round – they are the size of a squashed golf ball and have little leaves on the stalky bit. I always tend to parboil my turnips for 5 minutes to soften them and take away the rawness. This also makes them more absorbent to flavours. Turnips love tarragon, rosemary, thyme, bay leaves, olive oil, radicchio and bitter leaves. These turnip dishes are great as part of an antipasti plate, eaten hot or cold with cured meats like bresaola or prosciutto. Also fantastic with all roasted meats, or with fish like salmon and trout.

BOILED TURNIPS WITH THYME BEURRE BLANC

SERVES 4
400g small turnips
olive oil
50g unsalted butter, cubed
6 tablespoons herb vinegar

1 wineglass of white wine
½ a bunch of fresh thyme, leaves
   picked and smashed

Parboil the turnips, drain, then put them back in the pan with 3 tablespoons of oil and half the butter and cook until golden. Pour in the herb vinegar and scrape all the goodness off the bottom of the pan, then add the wine, the rest of the butter and the thyme. Simmer until the wine and butter have reduced, giving you a creamy, emulsified sauce that coats the turnips – this normally takes a couple of minutes. Season carefully to taste and serve straight away.

THE BEST ROASTED TURNIPS

SERVES 4
400g small turnips
1 bunch of fresh thyme or
   rosemary, leaves picked
6 tablespoons white wine or
   herb vinegar
olive oil

1 knob of unsalted butter
optional: 8 slices of prosciutto
optional: ½ a head of radicchio
   or other bitter leaves
optional: balsamic vinegar

Parboil the turnips, drain, then put them into a large ovenproof frying pan with a pinch of sea salt and black pepper, the herbs and the vinegar. Drizzle over 2 tablespoons of oil, dot them with butter, and roast at 220°C/425°F/gas 7 until golden. Give the pan a shake and serve straight away.

Or you can try something I did the other day, which was superb. Simply lay some prosciutto slices, so they overlap, over the frying pan once the turnips are cooked. Dress some radicchio or bitter leaves with balsamic vinegar and place these over the prosciutto. Roast for 5 minutes, or until the prosciutto is crispy. Remove the prosciutto to plates and serve the turnips on top.

CARROTS

Carrots are brilliant. In the last year or so we've been lucky enough to have seen lots of different varieties of carrots available in the shops – long, round, peculiar-shaped, and even some purple ones. My favourite ways of cooking carrots all serve 4 people – for each recipe you will need 500g of carrots, either left whole if they are baby ones, or sliced into small erratic pieces.

CARROTS BOILED WITH ORANGE, GARLIC & HERBS

Boil the carrots in boiling salted water, with a knob of unsalted butter and a little handful of fragrant herbs, tied up. Parsley, rosemary, thyme, bay – use just one or a mixture. Cut an orange into eighths and add to the water, along with a few whole garlic cloves in their skins. If you really want to be a little tiger, add a pinch of cumin as well (seeds or ground) – it subtly cuts through with the most wonderful flavour. As soon as the carrots are cooked, drain, discarding the herbs and all but one of the orange pieces. Squeeze the garlic out of its skin, chop the remaining orange piece finely and toss with the carrots, some sea salt and black pepper and a little more butter.

ROASTED CARROTS WITH ORANGE, GARLIC & THYME

Or – just as easy – as soon as you drain the carrots you can throw them into a baking tray with the chopped-up orange and the garlic cloves and roast them at 200°C/400°F/gas 6 for 10 minutes – this will give you a slightly meatier flavour.

MASHED CARROTS

Mash the carrots with the orange and garlic, so you have a mixture of coarse and smooth.

SWEETCORN

Sweetcorn is a great vegetable – most people love it. A source of vitamin C, it's not only tasty but helps to keep our immune system healthy. I'm not averse to using a bit of tinned sweetcorn sometimes, as it does taste OK, but I'd like you to buy some corn on the cob and have a go at removing the kernels yourself. It's very easy; just tear the husk off, then run a knife downwards to remove the kernels – it's definitely worth doing this to experience the sweetness and vibrancy of flavour. Sweetcorn is best served simply. It is massively in love with butter, has tendencies to flirt with the chilli family and loves a bit of bittersweet orange zest.

SWEETCORN WITH BUTTER, SALT & PEPPER

The simplest way to cook sweetcorn is in a pan with a good knob of unsalted butter, sea salt and black pepper. Place the lid on top and cook on a medium heat for 8 to 10 minutes, or until you have beautiful tender sweetcorn, that's juicy and soft. A wonderful way to cook it.

STIR-FRIED CORN WITH CHILLI, GINGER, GARLIC & PARSLEY

One of the other things I love to do is to stir-fry the kernels in a hot wok or frying pan with 2 tablespoons of olive oil, 1 tablespoon of finely chopped ginger, 1 teaspoon of finely chopped chilli, 1 handful of chopped fresh flat-leaf parsley and 2 tablespoons of low-salt soy sauce. You can vary the flavours with different herbs, but this is a good base to start with.

CREAMED CORN

Another dish you should try is this creamed sweetcorn. It's delicious, and a great alternative to mashed potato or polenta. First of all, cook 400g of corn in a pan with a good knob of unsalted butter, a wineglass of water and some crumbled, dried chilli. Cook with the lid on, on a medium heat, until tender. Place it in a food processor and blend until creamy and smooth. At this point you could add a little crème fraîche, but you may like it just as it is. Season to taste with sea salt and black pepper and serve, sprinkled with fresh baby mint leaves and orange zest.

BETTER

SPINACH

Spinach is a great leaf vegetable, whether you eat it cooked or use baby spinach raw in salads. It's worth remembering, though, that baby spinach doesn't have the depth of flavour that older spinach has. It is best friends with garlic, marjoram, nutmeg and cream. Spinach is a source of Vitamin A, which helps keep our immune system healthy, pluc Vitamin C, which acts as an antioxidant to protect our cells from damage. Mature spinach contains four times the beta-carotene of broccoli, so is very good for you! It also contains high levels of folic acid, which can help to reduce tiredness. It is one of the simplest vegetables in the world to cook as it literally takes 1 minute, but I'm still amazed that people will boil it for 5 minutes or more. This will leave the spinach grey, with all the green goodness left in the water. So make sure you don't do this – it's madness! Don't be fooled by spinach, though – by the time you've cooked it it will be a fraction of the size it started out as. So always use twice as much as you think you need. As a general guide I would suggest 100g per person.

PERFECT BRAISED SPINACH

The simplest way to cook spinach is in a pan with a little olive oil, unsalted butter, a grating of nutmeg and a tiny squeeze of lemon juice with a lid on to steam. This goes with just about anything – pasta, fish or meat. If there is any excess moisture when the spinach is cooked, just tilt the pan so it runs to the other side and pour it away. Let the spinach sit for 1 minute, then serve.

WONDERFUL CREAMED SPINACH

The second way I like to cook spinach is fairly similar to the braised method above. To serve 4 people, use 400g of spinach, follow the recipe above but simply add some double cream and 15g of freshly grated Parmesan cheese. Either stir, bring to the boil and serve, or pop in a dish and bake in a hot oven at 200°C/400°F/gas 6 for 10 minutes, or until just coloured on top.

CURRIED SPINACH

For this dish, all you need to do is melt 2 knobs of unsalted butter in a large pan and slowly fry ½ a teaspoon of ground coriander and ½ a teaspoon of garam masala. Add 2 finely sliced cloves of garlic, 1 teaspoon of mustard seeds, 1 finely sliced fresh red chilli, 1 pinch of ground cumin and 1 handful of fresh or dried curry leaves, if you can get them. (Don't worry if you can't, but they are great.) Add the spinach and cook down until any liquid has disappeared and the spinach is almost black. Indian chefs often cook this to eat with paneer, which is an Indian cheese a bit like halloumi, but I've eaten it just with some boiled potatoes and finished with a tiny squeeze of lemon juice.

JERUSALEM ARTICHOKES

Jerusalem artichokes are sweet and almost garlicky and mushroomy and gorgeous. Although called artichokes, they're actually tubers – like rough and ready potatoes. You can scrub and roast them whole like mini jacket potatoes, split them open and drizzle with a little chilli oil. You can even use them in a salad with smoky bacon. A Jerusalem artichoke's best friends are sage, thyme, butter, bacon, bay, cream, breadcrumbs, cheese and anything smoked.

SAUTÉED JERUSALEM ARTICHOKES WITH GARLIC & BAY LEAVES

To serve 4, you will need 600g of Jerusalem artichokes. Peel, then cut them into chunks. Place in an oiled frying pan and fry on a medium heat until golden on both sides, then add a few bay leaves, 2 cloves of garlic, peeled and finely sliced, 1 splash of white wine vinegar, some salt and pepper, and place a lid on top. After about 20 to 25 minutes they will have softened up nicely and you can remove the lid and the bay leaves. Continue cooking for a couple of minutes to crisp the artichoke chunks up one last time, then serve straight away. Personally, I think they go well with both meat and fish and are particularly good in a plate of antipasti, or in soups or warm salads.

SMASHED SAUTÉED JERUSALEM ARTICHOKES WITH PANCETTA & SAGE

To cook them this way, follow the recipe above but once you've removed the lid and the bay leaves, push the Jerusalem artichokes to one side and fry 8 slices of chopped smoked bacon or pancetta with 1 handful of sage leaves until crispy. Stir everything together until you have a wonderful mixture of chunky and mashed artichokes with crispy sage and bacon. Season to taste with sea salt and black pepper.

GRATINATED ARTICHOKES

There are two ways in which you can do this. You can either cook the artichokes as in the first recipe above and add a little cream and grated Parmesan cheese to the pan at the end. Or you can boil the sliced artichokes until cooked and softened, then drain and allow to steam with the lid on for a few minutes. Get a pan hot and fry the artichokes in a little unsalted butter and some thyme until golden. Stir in a wineglass of cream and a little grated Parmesan. By this time the artichokes should be like a chunky mash. I then like to dress 2 handfuls of picked sage leaves with a little olive oil, and I sprinkle these over the top. Either way, you need to pop the pan into a hot oven at 200°C/400°F/gas 6 for 8 to 10 minutes, or until the sage is crispy.

PEPPERS

Peppers are great. They make me feel summery and happy, and the thing I like most about them is their wonderful sweetness. The thing I hate about them, however, is their skin, which can sometimes be quite thick. The ultimate way to remove the skin is on a barbecue, or to hold the peppers with a pair of tongs directly over a flame on the stove until the skins are black. Place the peppers in a covered bowl, allow to sit and steam for 15 minutes, then simply peel the skin off. However, if you prick the peppers all over with a fork, put them in a jug covered with clingfilm and pop them into the microwave for a couple of minutes, after 10 minutes' cooling time you can normally remove the skins easily. Be very careful when you take them out, as the steam inside will be very hot. The peppers will still taste sweet doing it this way, but you won't get the lovely charred flavour you get from blackening them.

Peppers go well with loads of things, but their best friends are garlic, basil, tomatoes, onions, herbs, anchovies, capers, oils, balsamic or herb vinegars ... basically peppers are right old tarts – they get round a bit! Peppers are super-high in Vitamin C, which keeps our skin and teeth healthy and acts as an antioxident to protect our cells from damage. They are also a good source of folic acid, so are good to eat if you are trying to get pregnant or in the early stages of pregnancy. Peppers can be treated as salads, tossed with pasta, stirred into risottos, used with rice, potatoes, most meats and most fish. Roasted, marinated peppers are lovely as part of an antipasti dish. You can get various colours of pepper, but the red ones, which have been left to mature for longer, are the sweetest.

MARINATED PEPPERS

Once you've peeled some red, yellow or green peppers, halve, deseed and cut into 2.5cm-thick slices. Slowly fry in some olive oil with a couple of cloves of peeled and finely sliced garlic, one peeled and finely sliced red onion and ½ a bunch of fresh sliced basil. You don't have to brown the garlic or onions, you can just fry them for a couple of minutes to soften or you can give them just a little bit of colour, which is nice. Either way, put them in a bowl, correct the seasoning with sea salt and black pepper, and then add a swig or two of wine or balsamic vinegar to give a marvellous twang. Serve sprinkled with a few whole basil leaves.

SPANISH-STYLE PEPPERED POTATOES

Parboil 800g of peeled and diced potatoes in boiling salted water for 10 minutes, then drain and leave to steam for a few minutes with a lid on. You will need the same amount of sliced marinated peppers (roughly 4 peppers, prepared as recipe above). While the potatoes are still steaming, dress with the marinade from the peppers and pop into a heatproof dish or baking tray. Sprinkle with sea salt, black pepper, 1 teaspoon of smoked paprika and 1 teaspoon of finely sliced red chilli. Place the potatoes in the oven at 200°C/400°F/gas 6 until golden, then pour over the marinated peppers and give the potatoes a good shifty about so the peppers are well mixed in. Put back into the oven for 5 to 10 minutes, or until golden and perfect.

the dinner ladies from
kidbrooke: nora, viv,
george, chris and anne

PEAS

Fresh peas are one of the real joys of the world – there's something wonderful about the taste of freshly podded peas served simply with a little unsalted butter. Unless you live in the countryside, and can grow your own, this opportunity has become rarer and rarer, but to the credit of commercialization, frozen peas still remain in the top ten of some of the things that we produce well in large quantities.

EASY PEAS

Whether you're using fresh or frozen peas, for 4 people you need to put 4 good handfuls of peas into a wide frying pan or casserole pan with a lid (or you can use tin foil), with ½ a wineglass of white wine, ½ a wineglass of water and 2 good knobs of unsalted butter. Place the lid on top and bring to the boil, then remove the lid and simmer for 1 to 2 minutes while you finely slice ½ a bunch of picked mint leaves. With this reasonably small amount of liquid, the butter and wine should form a fantastically simple sauce. Throw in the mint at the last minute and serve straight away. Don't forget that it only takes 1 handful of freshly grated Parmesan cheese and some cooked tagliatelle to turn these peas into a wonderful pasta dish. Or you can add them to a risotto, or whiz them up with some chicken stock to make a fine pea soup.

FRENCH-STYLE PEAS

This isn't the classic French way of doing it, but peas and lettuce are wonderful together. People often think you can't cook lettuce, but it becomes wonderfully sweet. For 4 people you will need 4 good handfuls of fresh or frozen peas, 6 rashers of smoked streaky bacon, 2 gem lettuces, 2 knobs of unsalted butter and some chicken or veg stock. First, finely slice the bacon and fry in a little oil until golden and crisp. Add the peas and the gem lettuce, finely sliced. Mix up well, cover with 140ml of chicken stock, then simmer for 15 minutes, or until tender, removing the lid for the last 5 minutes to let the liquid reduce a little. Remove from the heat and add the butter. This will make the juice really creamy and oozy. Check the seasoning and serve straight away.

Pasta has always had a really important place in the kitchen, whether it's in a posh restaurant, in a school or when you're living on a budget in your first place. That's the time when it was most important to me, because I wanted to eat well but economically, too. So what I've done in this chapter is concentrate on all the cheap, accessible, hearty dishes that are great for making at home, or for large numbers of people. One thing I have noticed is that here in Britain people tend to use lots of sauce on their pasta, whereas in Italy only a small amount is used – just enough to lightly cover the 'star' of the dish: the pasta!

I've focused on dried pasta rather than fresh, as it's one of those store cupboard items that's available all the time, just waiting to be used. There are some dishes included here that only take a few minutes to make, and others that can be baked in the oven and take a little longer. All are really comforting, easy to make and not particularly expensive, so have a go. I'm sure you'll love them all.

PASTA BIANCA

To kick this section off we're going to start with the most basic dish to make, using the simplest sauce – Pasta Bianca means 'white pasta'. When it comes to grating the garlic, I suggest you do this using a fine grater. The slices will almost turn into a paste when you fry them. You can use any kind of pasta, but classically it's made with fresh tagliatelle or tagliolini. This recipe gives you a really good feel for how to cook pasta properly – you want the sauce to just coat the pasta and not to be too claggy or sticky. If we ever have kids eating at the restaurant and they're a little fussy, they always tend to go for this, with a little bit of freshly grated Parmesan cheese on the top.

This dish can also be quite luxurious. It's the key pasta dish that's made when white truffles are in season. The truffles are literally sliced over the top – I can't think of anything nicer to have with them than really cheesy, buttery pasta.

SERVES 6
2 cloves of garlic, peeled and finely grated
40g unsalted butter
450g dried tagliatelle
2 or 3 handfuls of freshly grated Parmesan cheese,
    plus extra to serve

In a small shallow pan, slowly fry the grated garlic in the butter without colouring for a couple of minutes. Cook the tagliatelle in a large pan of boiling salted water, according to the packet instructions. Once done, drain, reserving some of the starchy cooking water. Reserving this water and using it to finish off any pasta sauce is absolutely critical, especially this one.

Pour the melted garlic butter into a large warmed bowl so that the whole surface is covered, then toss in the cooked pasta with about 5 or 6 tablespoons of the reserved cooking water and the Parmesan cheese. Season to taste with sea salt and black pepper. With some tongs, or two forks, toss the pasta around – the butter, garlic, water and Parmesan will form a really creamy sauce.

What you need to do next is get everyone round the table. You may have to keep feeding the pasta with a little of the reserved cooking water, so the sauce stays silky and delicate and not too sticky. Once you get the consistency right, serve the pasta into bowls and pass round a big chunk of Parmesan cheese and a grater.

There are many ways of varying this sauce – you can lay some prosciutto over, or stir some chopped tomatoes into the garlic butter before removing from the heat, or you can incorporate different cheeses, but the key is to get simple, well-seasoned, delicate pasta coated in a butter and cheese sauce. Once you get this pasta exactly right, try to make it with a bit more speed next time – the quicker you can do it and get it right, the better the pasta will be.

CALORIES	FAT	SAT FAT	PROTEIN	CARBS	SUGAR	SALT	FIBRE
350kcal	9.7g	5.6g	12.3g	57.1g	1.7g	0.6g	0.1g

PASTA WITH SWEET TOMATO SAUCE & BAKED RICOTTA

This pasta dish uses a basic tomato sauce. The sweetness of it will depend on the quality of your tinned tomatoes. You should use whole tomatoes – don't buy pre-chopped ones, otherwise the seeds will add a bitterness to the sauce. The ricotta is baked separately with herbs and oil, then crumbled over the top – it's a really tasty recipe.

SERVES 6

450g ricotta cheese
olive oil
1 level teaspoon dried oregano
½ a dried red chilli, crumbled
1 onion, peeled and
    finely chopped
2 cloves of garlic, peeled and
    finely chopped
1 knob of unsalted butter

2 x 400g tins of quality plum
    tomatoes
3 tablespoons balsamic vinegar
450g dried pappardelle
1 bunch of fresh basil, leaves picked
    and torn
2 handfuls of freshly grated
    Parmesan cheese

Preheat the oven to 200°C/400°F/gas 6. Rub the ricotta all over with oil, sea salt, black pepper, the oregano and chilli, place on a baking tray, and roast for 20 minutes, or until golden and firm. In a pan, slowly fry the onion and garlic in the butter and a good drizzle of oil. Cook for 4 minutes, or until sweet and softened. Add the tomatoes, simmer gently for 15 minutes, then break the tomatoes up with a spoon. Add the balsamic and stir until you have a nice fine tomato sauce.

Meanwhile, cook the pappardelle in a large pan of boiling salted water, according to the packet instructions. Once done, drain, reserving some of the starchy cooking water. Toss the cooked pasta with the tomato sauce and add a little of the reserved water to loosen, if needed. Season carefully to taste, then, working quickly, add most of the basil and Parmesan cheese. Place in a warmed bowl, rip over some extra basil leaves, and grate over a little extra Parmesan. Crumble the baked ricotta over the pasta, or serve it at the table and let everyone crumble some over their plates.

CALORIES	FAT	SAT FAT	PROTEIN	CARBS	SUGAR	SALT	FIBRE
478kcal	15.1g	8.3g	21.3g	68.6g	12.4g	0.8g	2g

TAGLIATELLE WITH SPINACH, MASCARPONE & PARMESAN

Again, this is a good treat for kids. Even though they may not eat spinach on its own, I've never had a problem feeding this to my two-year-old. The reason she likes it so much is because she can suck on the spaghetti, and the mascarpone and cooking water make a fantastic sauce.

SERVES 6
450g dried tagliatelle or spaghetti
olive oil
2 teaspoons unsalted butter
2 cloves of garlic, peeled and sliced
1 whole nutmeg, for grating
400g baby spinach, finely sliced
120ml double cream
150g mascarpone cheese
2 handfuls of freshly grated Parmesan cheese

Cook the pasta in a large pan of boiling salted water, according to the packet instructions. Meanwhile, get a frying pan or wok hot, add a drizzle of oil, the butter and garlic, then grate in half the nutmeg. Once melted, add the spinach. After 5 minutes it will have wilted down and will be nice and dark. A lot of the liquid will have cooked away and you'll have wonderful intensely flavoured spinach. At this point, season with sea salt and black pepper until it tastes good, then add the cream, mascarpone and a little ladle of starchy cooking water from the pasta. Let this come to a simmer, then season again, if needed.

Drain the pasta, reserving some of the cooking water, then stir it into the spinach sauce. Add the Parmesan and toss everything together, then loosen to a nice silky consistency with some of the reserved cooking water, so it doesn't become too claggy. Serve straight away.

CALORIES	FAT	SAT FAT	PROTEIN	CARBS	SUGAR	SALT	FIBRE
339kcal	19.8g	10.3g	11.1g	31.1g	3.9g	0.8g	4.1g

SPAGHETTI WITH UNCOOKED TOMATO, ROCKET & OLIVE SAUCE

When you get home and you've got the munchies but no food planned, this is one of the quick things you can get done in ten minutes. The thing to remember is that you will get better results and a better flavour if your tomatoes are at room temperature before you begin.

SERVES 6
450g dried spaghetti
5 medium ripe tomatoes
1 bunch of fresh basil
1 good handful of tasty black or green olives,
    stone in
2 handfuls of fresh rocket
1 level teaspoon dried oregano, or ½ a bunch of fresh
    oregano, leaves picked and chopped
2 tablespoons balsamic vinegar
extra virgin olive oil

Cook the spaghetti in a pan of boiling salted water, according to the packet instructions. Gather your guests round the table and ask them to sort out drinks, plates and cutlery while you chop up the tomatoes and basil. You can do this any old way – little chunks, pulpy bits, just chop it all up. Squash the olives and remove the stones. Chop them up as well if you want to. Finely slice the stalky bits of the rocket and roughly chop the leaves. Put all these ingredients in a bowl with the oregano. Add the balsamic vinegar and 6 tablespoons of extra virgin olive oil, and season carefully with sea salt and black pepper. Taste and season, taste and season, until you get it spot on.

By now your pasta should be cooked, so drain it, reserving some of the starchy cooking water. Toss the pasta in the bowl with the tomatoes – you probably won't need to add any cooking water because the tomatoes are quite watery, but do add a little if you feel the sauce needs loosening slightly. Work quite fast, because it's the heat of the pasta that warms up the tomatoes and you don't want it to get cold. However, if it does get cold, all is not lost, as it makes a great pasta salad! Serve with some wine and a green salad. Knowing Italians, they'd have some crusty bread as well, and a nice bit of Parmesan or pecorino to grate over the top is a joy.

CALORIES	FAT	SAT FAT	PROTEIN	CARBS	SUGAR	SALT	FIBRE
389kcal	13.8g	2g	9.5g	60.5g	5.2g	0.6g	1.2g

RIGATONI WITH SWEET TOMATOES, AUBERGINE & MOZZARELLA

This is a dish I've had many times in Italy, on the Amalfi coast. It's one of those dishes that tastes like home – it's comfort food and it makes you feel good. The interesting thing about it is that it uses the firmer cow's milk mozzarella, which is torn up and thrown in at the last minute so that when you dig your spoon in you get melted, stringy bits of cheese – a real joy to eat. You can serve this as soon as it's made, or you can put it all into a baking tray with a little cheese grated on top and reheat it as a pasta bake the next day if you wish.

SERVES 6

1 firm ripe pink, black or
    white aubergine
olive oil
2 cloves of garlic, peeled
    and sliced
1 onion, peeled and
    finely chopped
2 x 400g tins of quality
    plum tomatoes
1 tablespoon balsamic vinegar

optional: 1–2 fresh or dried red chillies,
    chopped or crumbled
1 bunch of fresh basil, leaves picked
    and torn, stalks finely sliced
4 tablespoons double cream
450g dried rigatoni or penne
extra virgin olive oil
125g cow's milk mozzarella cheese
Parmesan cheese, for grating

Remove both ends of the aubergine and slice it into 1cm slices, then slice these across and finely dice into 1cm cubes. Some people prefer to season their aubergine with sea salt and let it sit for a while in a colander to draw out the bitterness, but I don't really do this unless I'm dealing with a seedy, bitter aubergine. This dish is really best made using a firm silky one.

Put a large pan on the heat and drizzle in 4 to 5 tablespoons of oil. Once hot, add the aubergine and stir to coat in the oil. Cook on a medium heat for 7 or 8 minutes, then add the garlic and onion and cook until lightly golden. Pour in the tomatoes and the balsamic vinegar, stir and season carefully with salt and black pepper. At this point, if you want to give the dish a little heat, you can add some chopped fresh or crumbled dried chilli, but that's down to you. Add the basil stalks and simmer the sauce nice and gently for 15 minutes, then add the cream.

Meanwhile, cook the rigatoni in a large pan of boiling salted water, according to the packet instructions, then drain, reserving some of the starchy cooking water. I like to put the pasta back into the pan it was cooked in with a tiny bit of the cooking water and a drizzle of extra virgin olive oil and move it around so it becomes almost dressed with the water and oil.

CALORIES	FAT	SAT FAT	PROTEIN	CARBS	SUGAR	SALT	FIBRE
509kcal	22.1g	8g	15.1g	66.9g	10.6g	0.3g	1.7g

At this point add the lovely tomato sauce to the pasta. By now the aubergines will have cooked into a creamy tomatoey pulp, which is just yum yum yum! Season carefully to taste with salt and pepper. When all my guests are sitting round the table, I take the pan to the table, tear up the mozzarella and the fresh basil, and fold these in for 30 seconds, then very quickly serve into bowls. By the time your guests start to eat, the mozzarella will have started to melt and will be stringy and gorgeous and really milky-tasting. Just lovely with the tomatoes and aubergine. Serve at the table with a block of Parmesan cheese and a grater so that everyone can help themselves.

FARFALLE WITH CARBONARA & SPRING PEAS

This is a twist on the classic carbonara, using spring peas and smoky bacon. A great combination and a big hit with the kids. My girls just love it.

SERVES 6
450g dried farfalle
1 large egg
100ml double cream
12 slices of pancetta or smoked streaky bacon, roughly sliced
3 handfuls of freshly podded or frozen peas
2 sprigs of fresh mint, leaves picked
2 handfuls of freshly grated Parmesan cheese

Cook the farfalle in a large pan of boiling salted water, according to the packet instructions. Whisk the egg in a bowl with the cream, sea salt and black pepper. Put the pancetta or bacon into a second pan and cook until golden and crisp.

When the farfalle is nearly cooked, add the peas for the last 2 minutes – this way they will be lovely and sweet. Once cooked, drain, reserving some of the starchy cooking water. Add the pasta to the pancetta, then finely slice and add most of the mint, reserving a few leaves for garnish.

Now you need to add the egg and cream mix to the pasta. What's important here is that you add it while the pasta is still steaming hot. This way, the residual heat of the pasta will cook the eggs, but not so that they resemble scrambled eggs, as I've seen in some dodgy old restaurants on the motorway! The pasta will actually cook the egg enough to give you a silky smooth sauce. Toss together and loosen with a little of the reserved cooking water, if needed. Season with salt and pepper, sprinkle with the Parmesan and the rest of the mint leaves, and serve immediately.

PS Work quickly for the best result.

CALORIES	FAT	SAT FAT	PROTEIN	CARBS	SUGAR	SALT	FIBRE
442kcal	17.8g	8.8g	15.4g	58.7g	2.8g	0.9g	0.9g

AWESOME SPINACH & RICOTTA CANNELLONI

This is such a wonderfully light and super-tasty cannelloni, and again I've avoided making the frustrating, painstaking béchamel sauce and given you a much tastier and simpler version. All you need to make sure of is that you fill the cannelloni well with the ricotta and spinach mix, so it's not all full of air. And the lovely thing about it is that it goes crispy and golden on top, but remains soft and moist at the bottom. You'll love it!

SERVES 8

2 knobs of unsalted butter

olive oil

2 cloves of garlic, peeled and finely sliced

1 big bunch of fresh marjoram or oregano, leaves picked and roughly chopped

1 whole nutmeg, for grating

8 large handfuls of baby spinach

1 bunch of fresh basil, leaves picked and torn, stalks chopped

2 x 400g tins of quality plum tomatoes, chopped

400g crumbly ricotta cheese

2 handfuls of freshly grated Parmesan cheese

16 cannelloni tubes

200g mozzarella cheese, broken up

WHITE SAUCE

500ml crème fraîche

3 anchovy fillets, in oil, finely chopped

2 handfuls of freshly grated Parmesan cheese

Preheat the oven to 180°C/350°F/gas 4. Find a metal baking tray or ovenproof dish that will fit the cannelloni in one layer so it's nice and snug – this way you'll get the right cover of sauce and the right amount of crispiness on top. When I cook this at home I just use one tray or pan to cut down on lots of washing up! Put the metal tray or a pan on a high heat and throw in the butter, add a drizzle of oil, one of the sliced garlic cloves and a handful of marjoram or oregano. Grate in a quarter of the nutmeg. By the time the tray is hot the garlic should be soft. Put as much spinach as will fit into the pan. Keep turning it over; it will wilt quickly so you will be able to keep adding more spinach until it's all in – the liquid will cook out of the spinach, which is fine. By cooking it this way you don't lose any of the nutrients that you would if boiling it in water.

After 5 minutes, put the spinach into a large bowl and leave to cool. Place the tray back on the heat, add a little oil, the other clove of sliced garlic, the basil stalks, tomatoes and 1 tin's worth of water. Bring to the boil, then turn the heat down. Add a pinch of sea salt and black pepper, then simmer for 10 minutes, or until you get a loose sauce consistency. Take the tray off the heat and stir in the basil leaves.

(Continued →)

By now the spinach will have cooled down, so squeeze any excess liquid out of it and pour this back into the bowl. Finely chop the spinach and put it back into the bowl. Mix it with the liquid, add the ricotta and 1 handful of the Parmesan, then use a piping bag to squeeze the mixture into the cannelloni. You can make your own piping bag by getting a sandwich bag and putting the spinach mix into the corner of it. Twist the bag up and cut the corner off, then carefully squeeze the filling into the cannelloni tubes so each one is filled right up – really easy.

Lay the cannelloni over the tomato sauce in the tray, or pour the tomato sauce into an ovenproof dish and lay the cannelloni on top. To make the white sauce, mix together the crème fraîche, anchovies and the 2 handfuls of Parmesan with a little salt and pepper, then loosen with a little water until you can spoon it over the cannelloni. Drizzle with oil, sprinkle with the remaining Parmesan and the mozzarella, and bake for 20 to 25 minutes, or until golden and bubbling.

CALORIES	FAT	SAT FAT	PROTEIN	CARBS	SUGAR	SALT	FIBRE
357kcal	23.5g	14.1g	14g	23.1g	7.3g	1g	1.9g

QUICK TOMATO MACARONI CHEESE

I think this is the best macaroni cheese recipe ever! This is a dish I make for the whole family, one that we all love to eat. I've used sweet tomatoes in my recipe as they really complement the cheese, and instead of béchamel I've used single cream, as it's a lot lighter. I've also topped the dish off with cheesy breadcrumbs, which give it a wonderful crunch. I think you'll laugh when you see how easy it is to make. I put it together extremely quickly by using my food processor. Don't worry if you haven't got one – you can chop it all by hand, then mix it in a bowl.

SERVES 6

360g dried macaroni

200g bread, preferably stale, for making breadcrumbs

800g super ripe tomatoes

1 clove of garlic, peeled

2 large handfuls of fresh basil, leaves picked

50g sun-dried tomatoes, chopped

2 anchovy fillets, in oil

3 handfuls of freshly grated Parmesan cheese

500ml single cream

1 tablespoon red wine vinegar

1 whole nutmeg, for grating

400g cow's milk mozzarella cheese, broken up

1 bunch of fresh thyme, leaves picked

olive oil

Preheat the oven to 200°C/400°F/gas 6. Cook the macaroni in a large pan of boiling salted water, according to the packet instructions. Meanwhile, break the bread up, place it in a food processor and whiz to breadcrumbs. Set aside. Place the tomatoes in the food processor with the garlic, basil, sun-dried tomatoes, anchovies and a good pinch of sea salt and black pepper. Whiz for 30 seconds, then add 2 handfuls of the Parmesan, the cream and vinegar and grate in half the nutmeg. Whiz until smooth and season to taste so it's really yummy!

By this time your macaroni will probably be cooked, so drain, reserving some of the starchy cooking water. Tip the pasta back into the pan and pour over every last bit of the cheesy sauce – you want it to be quite loose because you'll be surprised how quickly the sauce will disappear inside the macaroni and will look dry. Add a few spoonfuls of the reserved cooking water. Get yourself a baking dish about 8 to 10cm deep – this could be an earthenware dish or even a shallow ovenproof pan. Pour the pasta straight into the baking dish and break the mozzarella into little pieces over the top. Mix the last handful of Parmesan with the thyme leaves and breadcrumbs and sprinkle evenly over the top. Drizzle generously with olive oil – this will give you a lovely crunchy topping.

Bake for 20 to 25 minutes, or until piping hot and golden on top. Serve straight away, sprinkled with a little extra Parmesan. Best eaten with a nice salad – and you'll love it.

CALORIES	FAT	SAT FAT	PROTEIN	CARBS	SUGAR	SALT	FIBRE
556kcal	24.4g	13.5g	19.3g	68.8g	9.3g	1.7g	3g

WORKING GIRL'S PASTA

This is a pasta dish that Gennaro Contaldo used to make for our staff dinners when we worked at the Neal Street Restaurant in Covent Garden. In Italian this is called 'pasta puttana', which basically translates as 'whore's pasta'! I wanted to know why, as I'd never heard of this before. Maybe it's because the dish was cooked very quickly, with no effort involved, or maybe it's something the local prostitutes used to eat at home – who knows?!

But this is the way my darling Gennaro taught me to make it. He comes from the Amalfi coast, where fresh tuna would have been available. If you can get hold of some, it will make the dish much more luxurious and an event to eat. But if you can't, then tinned will do.

SERVES 6

1 handful of fresh basil
1 lemon
olive oil
2 x 225g tuna steaks, chopped into
    bite-sized chunks, or 2 tins of tuna
    in spring water
450g dried penne or spaghetti
8 anchovy fillets, in oil
2 cloves of garlic, peeled and
    finely chopped
2 handfuls of baby capers

1 handful of black olives, stone in
1–3 small dried red chillies, crumbled,
    to taste, or 1 fresh red chilli,
    deseeded and finely sliced
2 handfuls of ripe tomatoes,
    finely chopped
optional: 1 swig of white wine
1 bunch of fresh flat-leaf parsley,
    leaves picked and finely chopped

Smash the basil to a pulp with a pinch of sea salt and black pepper. Grate over the lemon zest and squeeze in the juice and pour in 2 good lugs of oil. Mix this up and either rub over the chopped fresh tuna or mix with your broken-up tinned tuna and allow to marinate.

Cook the pasta in a large pan of boiling salted water, according to the packet instructions. As soon as you put the pasta on, put 3 or 4 good lugs of oil into a large frying pan and put on the heat. As the pan starts to get warm, add the anchovy fillets and allow them to fry and melt. At this point add the garlic, capers, olives and chilli and stir around for 2 minutes. If using fresh tuna, add it to the pan now with all of the marinating juices and sear on all sides. Once done, add the tomatoes and a little swig of white wine if you have some. If you have used tinned tuna, add it to the pan at the same time as the tomatoes. Bring to the boil, then simmer for 5 minutes, stirring regularly with a spoon, breaking the tuna up into smaller pieces. What you don't want to do is overcook the tuna so it goes tough. You want it to be soft and silky. Taste and correct the seasoning with salt and pepper.

Drain the pasta, reserving some of the starchy cooking water. Toss the pasta with the sauce, add the parsley, then mix well – you may need an extra lug of oil and a spoonful of cooking water to make the sauce nice and loose.

CALORIES	FAT	SAT FAT	PROTEIN	CARBS	SUGAR	SALT	FIBRE
415kcal	8.7g	1.4g	29.5g	58.3g	2.6g	1.7g	0.4g

PASTA PEPERONATA

This is a great pasta dish using rigatoni, which is quite robust. It makes a really nice lunch. The mascarpone or crème fraîche is a lovely addition, but you can leave it out if you prefer. It will give you a wonderful mottled sauce, but try it without first and see how you go.

SERVES 6

2 red peppers, deseeded
   and sliced
2 yellow peppers, deseeded
   and sliced
olive oil
2 red onions, peeled and
   finely sliced
2 cloves of garlic, peeled and
   finely grated
1 bunch of fresh flat-leaf parsley,
   leaves picked and finely chopped,
   stalks finely chopped

2 tablespoons red wine or
   balsamic vinegar
2 handfuls of freshly grated Parmesan
   cheese
optional: 2 heaped tablespoons
   mascarpone or crème fraîche
450g dried rigatoni, penne or spaghetti
extra virgin olive oil

Put all the peppers in a large frying pan over a medium heat with a little olive oil and a pinch of sea salt and black pepper. Place a lid on, and cook slowly for 15 minutes, or until softened. Don't rush this too much, as cooking the peppers slowly like this really helps to bring out the flavour. Add the onion and cook for a further 20 minutes, then add the garlic and parsley stalks and toss around, keeping everything moving in the pan. Cook for 3 minutes more. Have a little taste, and season with a bit more salt and pepper. Add the vinegar – it will sizzle away, so give everything a good toss. Add one handful of the grated Parmesan and the mascarpone or crème fraîche (if using it) and turn the heat down to minimum while you cook the pasta.

Cook the rigatoni in a large pan of boiling salted water, according to the packet instructions. Once cooked, drain, reserving some of the starchy cooking water. Put the peppers, pasta and parsley leaves into a large warmed bowl. Toss together well, then add a little of the pasta cooking water and a few good lugs of extra virgin olive oil to coat the pasta nicely. Serve straight away, sprinkled with the remaining Parmesan.

CALORIES	FAT	SAT FAT	PROTEIN	CARBS	SUGAR	SALT	FIBRE
375kcal	7.1g	2.8g	14.8g	67.2g	11.7g	0.7g	4.9g

SWEET RED ONION PASTA

I was inspired to make this after hearing of a soup called 'carabaccia' that is flavoured with a stick of cinnamon. One of my students brought the recipe back from his work experience in Tuscany and it tastes amazing. So, on the same vibe, here's a pasta dish which I've made a little brothy – unusual but very nice. I would suggest using as many different varieties of onion as you can find.

SERVES 6

olive oil
2 large knobs of unsalted butter
2 white onions, peeled and sliced
3 red onions, peeled and sliced
1 clove of garlic, peeled and
    finely sliced
1 fresh red chilli, finely sliced
200g potatoes, finely sliced
½ a stick of cinnamon
½ a bunch of fresh thyme,
    leaves picked

1 whole nutmeg, for grating
450g dried fusilli or spaghetti
250ml quality chicken or vegetable stock
1–2 handfuls of freshly grated
    Parmesan cheese
1 bunch of fresh flat-leaf parsley,
    leaves picked and
    finely chopped

Put a drizzle of oil and the butter into a casserole pan and slowly fry the onions, garlic, chilli and potatoes with the cinnamon stick. Cook slowly for 5 minutes, then put the lid on and continue cooking for another 5 to 8 minutes, or until lightly golden. Add the thyme leaves and season carefully with sea salt, black pepper and a light grating of nutmeg.

Cook the fusilli in a large pan of boiling salted water, according to the packet instructions. Try one of the potatoes to check that it is soft (if not, you've made the slices too thick, but no worries – just add a little water to the pan and continue cooking until softened). Drain the pasta, reserving some of the starchy cooking water. Add the stock to the onions and mush up about half of the potatoes. Discard the cinnamon stick, then season to taste. Working quickly, toss the pasta with the onions and potatoes, loosening, if needed, with a little of the reserved cooking water, then add one or two handfuls of Parmesan and the parsley. When it's all nicely mixed together, serve up.

CALORIES	FAT	SAT FAT	PROTEIN	CARBS	SUGAR	SALT	FIBRE
442kcal	11.3g	5.9g	14.6g	75.3g	11.1g	1g	4.3g

opposite: ben arthur, loads of potential (fingers crossed)

WING

NECK

BA?

MEAT

FRONT
QUARTER

THIGH

HIND
QUARTER

WISHBONE

LEG

DRUMSTICK

HU

BREAST

BRISK

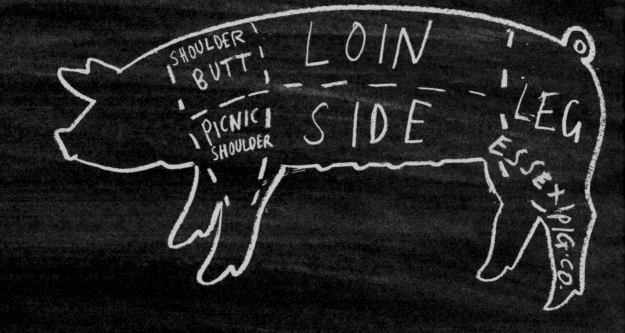

SHOULDER BUTT

PICNIC SHOULDER

LOIN

SIDE

LEG

ESSEX PIG CO.

RIB

SHORT RIB

SIRLOIN

RUN

SHORT LOIN

FEED ME FOOD · NOT MY FAMILY

ORGANIC FREE RANGE

When it comes to meat, always try to get the best you can afford. Although it's not always practical, it's great to know where your meat has come from, how it was raised, how long it was hung for and how it was butchered – build a relationship with your butcher and don't be afraid to ask him these things. Pale and pink meat, although it looks prettier than when it's a darker brown, just means that it has not been hung for very long, and it will always be far less tasty and far less tender. Also, don't be afraid of meat marbled with fat – it will have more flavour.

Even though I try not to preach too hard about it, I'm a great believer in using organic or free-range meat. I'd much rather eat a slow-cooked cheaper cut of organic meat that's been properly raised than have a more expensive fillet, or sirloin steak from God-knows-where, which will be tough with no flavour. If meat is organic, it means that the animal has been reared without the routine use of drugs and antibiotics, which are common in intensive livestock farming. My friend Patrick Holden, Director of the Soil Association, told me that all organic livestock products – from eggs to sausages to milk – are automatically free-range as this is a required standard. Free-range basically means that the animals aren't kept cooped up but are allowed to roam freely. I've come across quite a few skint students who have been cooking this way in their halls of residence really successfully. They have come to realize that they would rather spend their money on organic meat, so they choose cheaper cuts like brisket, shin, skirt and flank of beef, to name just a few.

Another thing to remember is that meat should be taken from the fridge in advance and allowed to reach room temperature before it's cooked – this will give you even cooking, and for the same reason it should also be allowed to rest after cooking, before carving or serving.

What I like about this chapter is that a lot of the dishes are very easy to prepare. I've taken a few cheap, ultra-accessible meats and with a little bit of imagination have created some fantastically economical dishes – which is what family food and home cooking are all about.

SUPER-TASTY SPANISH ROAST CHICKEN

This is a cracker of a dish to cook at home. It will really get your taste buds going as it fills the house with the most fantastic smells.

SERVES 8
1.6kg potatoes, peeled and cut into 2.5cm dice
4 lemons
1 x 2kg whole chicken
1 bunch of fresh flat-leaf parsley, leaves picked
   and finely chopped, stalks reserved
300g quality chorizo
olive oil
2 cloves of garlic, peeled and finely chopped

Preheat the oven to 220°C/425°F/gas 7, then place the potatoes with 2 of the lemons into a small pan of water and boil for 5 minutes. Drain, then prick the lemons all over with a knife. (The reason for doing this is that you are going to put them inside the chicken and their wonderful juices will be released while cooking. They will burst with flavour and fragrance, and the heat from the lemons will help the chicken to cook more quickly from the inside as well as making it taste and smell amazing.) Stuff the chicken with the hot lemons and the parsley stalks, then season the chicken and the potatoes with sea salt and black pepper, and slice the chorizo at an angle, ½cm thick.

Take a piece of greaseproof paper and wet it under a tap so it becomes flexible, then shake it out and lay it into an appropriately sized baking tray. Place the potatoes in the centre of the greaseproof, then place the chicken on top and sprinkle with the chorizo and a little of the chopped parsley. Drizzle with a little oil, then roast for 1 hour 20 minutes, or until golden and cooked through.

Meanwhile, make what the Italians call gremolata by finely chopping the zest of the 2 remaining lemons and mixing it with the chopped parsley and garlic. Season lightly and toss together to create a really fragrant seasoning-type garnish. Remove the tray from the oven, take the chicken out and put aside to rest. Give the potatoes a shake about and put them back in the oven for a few minutes to crisp up.

Carve the chicken and divide between plates, with the potatoes (they will have taken on the smoky paprika flavour from the chorizo, so if there's any juice left in the tray, pour every last drop over the plates). When you sprinkle over the gremolata it will hit the hot juice and smell fantastic. You're going to love this one! A rocket salad goes really well with it.

CALORIES	FAT	SAT FAT	PROTEIN	CARBS	SUGAR	SALT	FIBRE
439kcal	16.9g	5.7g	37.9g	36g	2.4g	1g	2.7g

BEST LAMB CUTLETS
WITH SPECIAL BASIL SAUCE

This dish is fantastic and can be ready in just over 5 minutes. Use either wild mushrooms that are in season, like girolles, trompettes de la mort and pieds de mouton, or more readily available farmed mushrooms like field, chestnut or oyster, as these are really tasty when cooked properly.

SERVES 4

12 lamb cutlets
½ a bunch of fresh thyme,
   leaves picked
olive oil
400g mixed mushrooms, torn
extra virgin olive oil

½ a bunch of fresh flat-leaf
   parsley, leaves picked
1 lemon
2 handfuls of pine nuts
1 big bunch of fresh basil
3–5 tablespoons balsamic vinegar

These lamb cutlets are best cooked on a hot barbecue with wood or charcoal, to give you a wonderful smoky flavour. Otherwise use a screaming hot griddle pan. Slap the cutlets with the heel of your hand to flatten slightly. Bash the thyme in a pestle and mortar and add a little oil. Mix together, then rub the oil over the cutlets and season both sides with sea salt and black pepper.

Cook the mushrooms dry on a hot griddle pan – this is quite an unusual way to do it, but it gives you a nutty flavour that you wouldn't get otherwise. Once the mushrooms are done, place in a bowl, then cook the lamb on the barbecue or griddle. If the cutlets are about 1.5cm thick, just give them 3 or 4 minutes on each side, or until they're really golden – this should cook them medium. (I'm not really into rare lamb cutlets, but if you prefer them like that, then cook for a little less time.)

Once cooked, put the cutlets into the bowl with the mushrooms and drizzle with a little extra virgin olive oil. Tear over the parsley, and add a good squeeze of lemon juice. Season lightly and toss together. Leave to rest and allow all the lovely juices to get sucked up by the mushrooms.

Meanwhile, make a really quick sauce. It looks a bit like pesto, but although it contains basil and pine nuts it's not very similar in flavour. Pound up the pine nuts in a pestle and mortar until you have a mushy pulp – this will give the sauce a creamy flavour and texture. Remove the mixture to a bowl, then bash the basil to a pulp. Add this to the pine nuts and loosen with extra virgin olive oil so that the sauce easily drops off the end of a spoon. Now you need to balance it with quite a lot of balsamic vinegar to give it a good zing, almost like a mint sauce, but add it to taste. Give the lamb and mushrooms a final toss. Serve up on a big platter and let everyone help themselves. Have the sauce and a simple watercress salad on the side.

CALORIES	FAT	SAT FAT	PROTEIN	CARBS	SUGAR	SALT	FIBRE
387kcal	27.5g	8.3g	29.3g	5.3g	4.4g	0.5g	1.4g

TRAYBAKED CHICKEN MARYLAND

This is a really quick and convenient dinner to make – great for Saturday nights with the family. Everyone I've cooked it for has loved it. It's kinda like an easy version of the southern American Maryland or, as many call it, 'sunshine' cooking. Although the idea of cooking chicken with sweetcorn and banana may sound grotesque to you, it really does work! Anyway, I've taken a few liberties in order to move this dish on to another level. You can use tinned sweetcorn, but remember that the flavour won't be anything near as good as fresh.

SERVES 4
4 fresh corn on the cob
1 x 400g tin of cannellini or butter beans, drained
4 skinless chicken breasts
2 ripe bananas, peeled
1 large wineglass of white wine
200ml double cream
50g unsalted butter
12 rashers of smoked streaky bacon or pancetta
1 bunch of fresh mint, leaves picked

Preheat the oven to 220°C/425°F/gas 7. Run a knife down the length of the raw corn cobs to remove the kernels – it takes no time at all to do this. Once done, add the corn to a roasting tray and discard the cobs. Using a fork (or your fingers!), squash up half the cannellini or butter beans until you have a pulp and add these, with the unsquashed half of the beans, to the tray.

The next thing to do is to put the chicken breasts on a chopping board. You will notice that each breast has a little strip or flap of meat on one side. Fold it back using a knife and make a cut to carefully form a little pocket inside the breast. Once you've done this to all 4 chicken breasts, squash half a banana into each pocket, then fold the flap back over to cover the banana. Season with sea salt and black pepper.

Turn the fillets the other way up and carefully place them on top of the corn and beans. Add the wine and double cream, then divide the butter into little knobs and scatter these all around the tray. Drape the bacon or pancetta slices over the chicken breasts and bake in the oven for 35 to 40 minutes, or until the bacon is crisp. The smoky flavour from the bacon and the smooth flavour of the bananas will have really cooked into the corn and the chicken. A lovely combination of flavours. Taste and correct the seasoning, if needed. I usually serve this in the dish at the table, with a handful of fresh mint thrown over, and let people help themselves.

CALORIES	FAT	SAT FAT	PROTEIN	CARBS	SUGAR	SALT	FIBRE
710kcal	38.6g	19.8g	45.9g	36.8g	14.4g	1.6g	5g

EVERYDAY CRISPY CHICKEN WITH SWEET TOMATOES

This recipe takes minutes to put together but then requires slow, gentle cooking. However, in return for your patience, what happens in the pan from just a couple of ingredients is an absolute joy and never fails, so it's a good one to serve if you have guests. Basically the skin of the chicken goes beautifully crisp and the meat becomes sticky and tender, while the tomatoes are slow-roasting and creating the most fabulous broth. The finished dish can be flaked into warm salads, tossed with some cooked and drained pappardelle or simply eaten as it is.

SERVES 4

4 chicken legs, jointed

1 big bunch of fresh basil, leaves picked, stalks finely chopped

2 big handfuls of ripe red and yellow cherry tomatoes, halved, and ripe plum tomatoes, quartered

1 whole bulb of garlic, broken up into cloves

1 fresh red chilli, finely chopped

olive oil

optional: 1 x 400g tin of cannellini beans, drained

optional: 2 handfuls of new potatoes

Preheat the oven to 180°C/350°F/gas 4. Season the chicken all over with sea salt and black pepper and put them into a snug-fitting pan in one layer. Throw in all the basil leaves and stalks, then chuck in the tomatoes. Scatter the garlic cloves into the pan with the chopped chilli and drizzle over some oil. Mix around a bit, pushing the tomatoes underneath. Place in the oven for 1 hour 30 minutes, or until the chicken skin is crisp and the meat falls off the bone, turning the tomatoes halfway. If you fancy, add some drained cannellini beans or some sliced new potatoes to the pan and cook them with the chicken, or serve the chicken with some simple mashed potato. Squeeze the garlic out of the skins before serving. You could even make it part of a pasta dish – remove the chicken from the bone and shred it, then toss into a bowl of linguine or spaghetti and serve at once.

CALORIES	FAT	SAT FAT	PROTEIN	CARBS	SUGAR	SALT	FIBRE
411kcal	20.4g	5.2g	31g	22.7g	2.2g	0.8g	8.1g

feed and love the
food that feeds you

ROASTED MARMALADE HAM

If you've got a family dinner or a party coming up, or you want to reinvent the Sunday roast, there's nothing outrageous about buying a ham and cooking it this way. You can feed loads of people and still have some left over for sarnies. There is something quite old English about this dish. It almost feels like something that would have been eaten at a royal banquet, it looks so sumptuous! But forgetting the romantic notions, the reason this combination is so genius is because through careful poaching you will get juicy meat, by sprinkling the meat generously with black pepper you will get a wonderful heat, and by covering the whole thing in marmalade you will get a beautiful tart sweetness. It really does make the most wonderful roast dinner.

SERVES 12

3–4kg middle-cut gammon, knuckle left on
2 carrots, roughly chopped
2 sticks of celery, roughly chopped
2 fresh bay leaves
16 black peppercorns

1 bouquet garni (a piece of leek, celery, a bay leaf, a sprig of fresh thyme)
2 oranges
1 jar of quality thin-rind marmalade
1 bunch of fresh rosemary, leaves picked

Place the gammon in a large but snug-fitting pot. Cover with water, then throw in the veg, bay leaves, peppercorns and bouquet garni. Peel the zest from the oranges and add to the water, then squeeze in the juice and add 2 tablespoons of sea salt. Bring to the boil, then turn the heat down and simmer for 1 hour 15 minutes with a lid on, skimming when needed. Remove from the heat and allow to cool for 30 minutes in the broth. This will allow the flavours to really penetrate the meat. Discard the vegetables from the broth, but keep the broth for making minestrone-type soups – it will freeze well for use another day.

Preheat the oven to 170°C/325°F/gas 3. Carefully remove the meat to a board and, using a knife, take off the skin. Depending on the breed and quality of the pig, you should have a nice layer of fat. Remove some of the fat as well, to leave you with about 1cm (the extra fat can be kept in the freezer for roasting with potatoes another time). Score the fat left on the meat in a criss-cross fashion, and season generously with 3 tablespoons of black pepper. Place the meat in a roasting tray and roast for 20 minutes, or until the fat renders and becomes slightly crispy. Remove from the oven, stir up the marmalade to loosen, then rub it all over the meat with the rosemary. Place back in the oven for 1 hour and baste frequently until beautifully golden and crisp. Serve as you would a roast dinner or as part of a picnic.

CALORIES	FAT	SAT FAT	PROTEIN	CARBS	SUGAR	SALT	FIBRE
445kcal	18.8g	6.2g	44g	26.4g	26.2g	5.7g	0.1g

GOOD OLD LIVER & BACON WITH A TWIST

Anything with liver in it always reminds me of my childhood. There were two things Dad wouldn't eat – one was rabbit, and the other was liver. And when it came to having liver for dinner, God bless my mum! She always used to cook the hell out of it and it would be quite chewy. And like all good food, dinner cooked by mothers is dinner cooked with a lot of love, so if it's not eaten, it can cause some upset. Mum would lecture Dad about how he should set an example to us and eat it. One day, it wasn't me or my sister who got told off for not eating our dinner – it was my poor old dad this time who refused to eat the liver she'd cooked. I don't remember what was said exactly, but I do remember, to our amusement, Mum picking up the *Royal Horticultural Society Gardeners' Encyclopaedia of Plants and Flowers* (not relevant, just handy and big) and chasing him round the kitchen with it. To which my dad very calmly sat down, 'tutted' and rolled his eyes. I've started doing this myself over the last five years – aargh – I'm turning into my dad! So, Mum and Dad, I dedicate this recipe to you and all heavy books.

SERVES 4

12 rashers of smoked streaky bacon
olive oil
½ a bunch of fresh sage leaves
600g calf's or lamb's liver, cleaned, trimmed and cut into strips
plain flour, for dusting
2 medium onions, peeled and finely sliced
4 tablespoons red or white wine vinegar
4 tablespoons unsalted butter

Get your biggest frying pan nice and hot. Add the bacon, cook until nice and crispy on both sides, then remove to a plate. Add a little oil to the bacon fat left in the pan, sprinkle in the sage leaves, and cook for 30 seconds – once crispy they give the most fantastic flavour and texture. Remove from the pan and put to one side with the bacon.

Dust the liver in a little flour, shaking off the excess, and place to one side. Cook the onions in the pan with a good pinch of sea salt for a few minutes, removing them once softened. Allow the pan to heat up once more with a drizzle of oil, then add the liver and cook in two batches over a really high heat for 1 minute on each side to caramelize and seal in the flavour – don't overcook the liver as it's nice to leave it a little pink. Put the onion, sage and bacon back into the pan with the vinegar, butter and all the liver. It will sizzle and spit, becoming creamy and saucy. Season to taste, and serve with buttery mashed potato mixed with loads of jarred, creamed or grated fresh horseradish. If you fancy, you can add a little cream or crème fraîche to make the mash nice and oozy.

CALORIES	FAT	SAT FAT	PROTEIN	CARBS	SUGAR	SALT	FIBRE
419kcal	25.1g	12.3g	36.5g	11.8g	5.8g	2.1g	2.3g

STIR-FRIED DUCK
WITH SUGAR SNAP PEAS & ASPARAGUS

Lots of people have woks, but so many people get it wrong because they don't really understand the principle of stir-frying – i.e. you get a pan really hot and you don't overcrowd it with veg so that it starts boiling and not stir-frying. You could make this with chicken breast instead, if that takes your fancy, or slices of pork. There are many ways you can vary this using different vegetables – try beansprouts, water chestnuts, spinach, courgettes or baby corn.

SERVES 4

4 duck breasts
2 teaspoons Chinese five-spice
2 tablespoons sunflower or
    groundnut oil
2 large handfuls of thin
    asparagus, trimmed
2 large handfuls of sugar
    snap peas or mangetout
4 cloves of garlic, peeled
    and finely sliced

1–3 fresh red chillies, deseeded
    and finely sliced
10 piece of ginger, peeled
    and finely grated
4 oranges, zested and segmented
1 tablespoon runny honey
1 bunch of fresh mint, leaves picked
4 tablespoons low-salt soy sauce

First of all, score the duck skin with a sharp knife, then dust all over with the five-spice and a good pinch of sea salt. Put the duck breasts skin side down in a cold wok, then bring it slowly up to a medium-low heat so the white fat turns into wonderful thin, crispy, golden crackling. Cook for 12 minutes, then turn the breasts over and cook for a further 5 minutes.

By this time they will be cooked medium, so remove to a plate and pour away the duck fat. Get all the veggies and flavourings ready to go and quickly wipe the wok. Now you want to get it really hot – if you want to open the window (and cover the fire alarm – joke!), then do. You may need to cook it all in smallish batches depending on the size of your wok.

Add 2 tablespoons of oil to the hot wok. Carefully swirl the oil around so that it covers the whole pan. Add the asparagus and sugar snap peas or mangetout and toss around, then add the garlic, chilli and ginger. Continue stir-frying on the highest heat for 2 minutes, or until the asparagus has softened a little but still has a nice crunch. Remove the veg to a plate. Slice up the duck breasts into little slivers and put these back into the wok with any resting juices and maybe an extra pinch of five-spice. Cook until nice and crispy.

Put all the vegetables back into the wok, and turn down the heat. Add the oranges, honey, half the mint and the soy sauce, and serve straight away on a large plate, sprinkled with the rest of the mint. Delicious served with rice or noodles, as a starter or main course.

CALORIES	FAT	SAT FAT	PROTEIN	CARBS	SUGAR	SALT	FIBRE
802kcal	70.4g	19g	26g	17.7g	16.5g	1.6g	3g

SPRING POACHED CHICKEN

To be honest, I think this has got to be one of my favourite meals, but at the same time none of my friends would even think about having poached chicken for dinner. It sounds boring, doesn't seem like much fun and it might even sound a bit healthy (which it is!). But do you know what, this is one of the most truly brilliant meals. People I've fed it to have been gobsmacked and I'm sure you will be, too. So please, trust me, I won't stitch you up. Have a go!

SERVES 6

1 x 2kg whole chicken
1 bunch of fresh flat-leaf parsley
4 fresh bay leaves
2 handfuls of new potatoes
2 handfuls of baby carrots
2 handfuls of baby turnips or radishes
1 bulb of fennel, quartered, herby
   tops reserved
freshly grated horseradish

optional: 1 jar hot creamed
   horseradish
250ml crème fraîche
2 handfuls of fresh peas
2 handfuls of broad beans
1 colanderful of spinach or Swiss chard
extra virgin olive oil
optional: 1 small handful of pale inner
   celery leaves

You will need a large casserole or stock pot to fit your chicken in so that you can cover it with water by about 2.5cm. Stuff the chicken with the parsley and bay leaves, then place the chicken in the pot, cover with water and add 1 good teaspoon of sea salt. Scatter in the potatoes, bring to the boil, then turn down the heat, place a lid on top and simmer for 20 minutes. At this point you can add the baby carrots, turnips or radishes and fennel. Carry on simmering for 30 to 40 minutes.

When you can easily pull the leg bone away from the chicken, you know that it's cooked to perfection. By that time the other veg will certainly be cooked, but don't break them up. Now ... while this is all cooking, you can prepare the horseradish cream – the most joyous thing to have with the chicken. In your supermarket you will be able to find creamed or hot grated horseradish in a jar, which is OK to use, but if you're really lucky, you'll be able to get hold of some fresh horseradish which you can simply peel and grate, season with salt and mix with the crème fraîche.

All you have to do now is carefully remove the chicken to a bowl and add the peas, broad beans and spinach to the broth. Allow them to cook for 1 minute, then season carefully to taste. You can get all your guests to help themselves if that's easier, but if you want to serve it up, divide a nice mixture of veg between 4 bowls, put some shredded chicken on top, then ladle over some of the wonderful, comforting broth. Sprinkle over some of the chopped reserved fennel tops or some celery leaves (if using), with a healthy dollop of horseradish crème fraîche on top and a drizzle of nice peppery extra virgin olive oil – it will look and taste brilliant.

CALORIES	FAT	SAT FAT	PROTEIN	CARBS	SUGAR	SALT	FIBRE
292kcal	13.9g	4.7g	38.1g	3.7g	1.4g	0.9g	1.7g

SWEET DUCK LEGS COOKED WITH PLUMS & STAR ANISE

If you're the type of person who goes into a supermarket and buys prepacked chicken or duck breasts, thighs or drumsticks, then I really want to start you thinking along the lines of buying a whole chicken or duck. It's far better to buy the whole bird and then remove the breasts or legs. I've also noticed that duck legs aren't as popular, because the packs of duck legs never seem to shift from the supermarket shelves like the chicken ones do – which is strange, because all they need is some slow cooking and you'll get thin crispy skin and beautiful melt-in-your-mouth meat. Check out this recipe, which works a real treat.

SERVES 4
4 fat duck legs
4 tablespoons low-salt soy sauce
3 teaspoons Chinese five-spice
1 handful of star anise
½ a stick of cinnamon
olive oil
1–2 fresh chillies, deseeded and sliced
16 plums, halved and destoned
2 tablespoons Demerara sugar

Place the duck legs in a sandwich bag with the soy sauce, five-spice, star anise, cinnamon stick and 1 tablespoon of oil and let them marinate for a minimum of 2 hours. To really get the flavours going, you could keep this in your fridge to marinate for up to 2 days. Preheat the oven to 170°C/325°F/gas 3, then get yourself a pan, casserole or high-sided roasting tray that snugly fits the duck legs. Place the chillies, plums and sugar in the bottom of the tray and pour the marinade from the bag over the top. Mix it all up using your fingers, and place the duck legs on top.

Place the tray in the oven for 2 to 2 hours 30 minutes, or until the meat falls away from the bone. Remove the star anise and cinnamon stick, then taste and adjust the seasoning, if needed. It's now down to you how you would like to serve it. You could have it as a starter with some of the little Chinese pancakes that you can buy, or served simply with rice or noodles and the chunky, jammy plum sauce that the duck has cooked in.

CALORIES	FAT	SAT FAT	PROTEIN	CARBS	SUGAR	SALT	FIBRE
500kcal	36.5g	10.3g	19.1g	25.9g	25.9g	1.6g	3.1g

JOOLS'S FAVOURITE BEEF STEW

Jools goes mad for this stew in the colder months of the year, and the kids love it, too. It's a straightforward beef stew to which all sorts of root veg can be added. I really like making it with squash and Jerusalem artichokes, which partly cook into the sauce, making it really sumptuous with an unusual and wonderful flavour.

The great thing about this stew is that it gets put together very quickly, and this is partly to do with the fact that no time is spent browning the meat. Even though this goes against all my training, I experimented with two batches of meat – I browned one and put the other straight into the pot. The latter turned out to be the sweeter and cleaner-tasting, so I've stopped browning the meat for most of my stews these days.

SERVES 4

olive oil

1 knob of unsalted butter

1 onion, peeled and chopped

½ a bunch of fresh sage, leaves picked

800g stewing steak or beef skirt,
    cut into 5cm pieces

plain flour, for dusting

2 parsnips, peeled and quartered

4 carrots, peeled and halved

½ a butternut squash, deseeded and
    roughly diced

optional: 1 handful of Jerusalem
    artichokes, peeled and halved

500g small potatoes

2 tablespoons tomato purée

½ a bottle of red wine

300ml quality beef or vegetable stock

1 lemon

½ a bunch of fresh rosemary, leaves
    picked and chopped

1 clove of garlic, peeled and finely
    chopped

Preheat the oven to 160°C/300°F/gas 2. Put a little oil and the butter into a large casserole pan. Add the onion and all the sage leaves and fry for 3 or 4 minutes. Toss the meat in a little seasoned flour, then add it to the pan with all the vegetables, the tomato purée, wine and stock, and gently stir together. Season generously with black pepper and just a little sea salt. Bring to the boil, place a lid on top, then cook in the oven until the meat is tender. Sometimes this takes 3 hours, sometimes 4 – it depends on what cut of meat you're using and how fresh it is. The only way to test is to mash up a piece of meat and if it falls apart easily, it's ready. Once it's cooked, you can turn the oven down to about 110°C/225°F/gas ¼ and just hold it there until you're ready to eat.

The best way to serve this is by ladling big spoonfuls into bowls, accompanied by a glass of French red wine and some really fresh, warmed bread. Finely grate the lemon zest, mix with the rosemary and garlic and sprinkle over the stew before eating. Just the smallest amount will make a world of difference – as soon as it hits the hot stew it will release an amazing fragrance.

CALORIES	FAT	SAT FAT	PROTEIN	CARBS	SUGAR	SALT	FIBRE
662kcal	20.2g	8.4g	52.2g	55.9g	22.7g	2g	11g

if daisy's crying,
watching me cooking
always stops her – could
this be a sign of potential?

LAMB WITH CHICKPEAS, YOGHURT & ROASTED VEG

Leg of lamb is a real favourite in British households, but I want to give you a totally different take on it. When buying your leg of lamb from the butcher, ask for it to be butterflied and opened out. This gives you a piece of meat that can be fried, grilled or cooked on the barbecue, because it's tender enough. It also allows it to be wonderfully marinated so it can take on great flavours, and it cooks much quicker than a normal leg of lamb. The flavours in this recipe are Moroccan-based. It's not an authentic Moroccan recipe, but it does taste really good and that's enough for me.

SERVES 6

1 x 2kg leg of lamb, bone out, butterflied and opened up like a book (ask your butcher)
2 teaspoons coriander seeds
3 cloves of garlic, peeled and finely chopped
1 big bunch of fresh coriander, leaves picked and chopped
1 big bunch of fresh mint, leaves picked and chopped
1 x 400g tin of chickpeas, drained

½ a lemon
500g natural yoghurt
12 baby turnips
1 bunch of baby carrots, tops left on
1 butternut squash, deseeded and cut into 8 wedges
2 red onions, peeled and quartered
1 whole bulb of garlic, broken into cloves
2 teaspoons ground cumin
olive oil

Score the lamb on both sides. Using either a pestle and mortar or a food processor, grind or whiz the coriander seeds with the peeled garlic cloves, coriander, mint and half the chickpeas until you have a paste. Season with sea salt and black pepper, then add the lemon juice and yoghurt. Put half the flavoured yoghurt into a large plastic bag and add the lamb. Put the other half of the flavoured yoghurt in the fridge. Tie the bag up to seal and turn it around to allow the yoghurt to coat all the lamb. Leave to marinate for at least 1 hour, preferably overnight in the fridge.

Preheat the oven to 200°C/400°F/gas 6. Place the turnips and carrots in a roasting tray with the squash, onions, unpeeled garlic cloves and remaining chickpeas, then sprinkle with the cumin, salt and pepper. Drizzle with oil and toss together to coat. Remove the lamb from the marinade, then place the meat directly on the oven rack with the tray of vegetables on the shelf below. Cook for 1 hour, tossing the vegetables halfway. Serve the lamb with the veg and flavoured yoghurt.

CALORIES	FAT	SAT FAT	PROTEIN	CARBS	SUGAR	SALT	FIBRE
452kcal	19.3g	7.2g	39.4g	33.4g	20g	0.8g	7.3g

SLOW-ROASTED SPICED PORK LOIN
WITH BLACK-EYED BEANS & TOMATOES

This dish works as described here, but you can also stuff it into hot flour tortillas or pitta breads to be eaten like a kind of fajita or burrito – superb. Spanish smoked paprika is now widely available, and your butcher can do the trimming and scoring of the pork loin for you to save you some time.

SERVES 8

2kg rib-end loin of pork, skin on,
  French-trimmed
5 teaspoons smoked paprika
1 lemon
olive oil
3 red onions, peeled and finely sliced
6–8 fresh red, yellow and green chillies
120g small whole chorizo sausages,
  thickly sliced
6 fresh bay leaves
2 sprigs of fresh rosemary, leaves
  picked and finely chopped

3 x 400g tins of quality plum
  tomatoes, roughly chopped
2 handfuls of ripe tomatoes, halved
4 x 400g tins of black-eyed
  beans, drained
5 cloves of garlic, peeled
  and finely chopped
1 bunch of fresh flat-leaf parsley,
  leaves picked and chopped
red wine vinegar
soured cream, to serve

Preheat the oven to full whack (240°C/475°F/gas 9). First, score the skin of the pork in a criss-cross pattern every 1cm with a sharp knife, trying not to cut into the meat itself. Mix a little sea salt with 1 teaspoon of paprika, the lemon juice and a little oil, then rub over the meat and into the score lines. Place in a high-sided roasting tray and cook for 30 minutes to start crisping the skin.

Remove the meat from the oven, turning the heat down to 180°C/350°F/gas 4. Take the pork out of the tray and put it to one side, then spoon away half the fat. Place the tray on the hob, add the onions, whole chillies, chorizo, bay leaves and rosemary with the remaining paprika, and fry gently until the onions are soft. Add all the tomatoes, the beans, garlic, parsley and a wineglass of water, stirring and scraping up all the lovely sticky bits from the bottom of the tray. Place the pork on top, and return to the oven for 50 minutes, or until cooked through, with crispy cracking.

Once cooked, remove the pork from the tray and allow to rest for 30 minutes. Taste the sauce and season with salt, pepper and a few swigs of red wine vinegar to give it a twang. Remove the chillies and control the heat by chopping up as much chilli as you like and stirring it back into the sauce. Lovely served with soured cream.

CALORIES	FAT	SAT FAT	PROTEIN	CARBS	SUGAR	SALT	FIBRE
906kcal	51.5g	18.5g	53.8g	46.8g	10.5g	1.2g	15.6g

ANDY THE GASMAN'S STEW

You might have heard me talking about my mate Andy the Gasman – he's the one who didn't ever want to use his oven as he thought it might devalue the price of his house, so he left it in its cellophane wrapper! Five years on and nothing's changed, but I wanted to get him cooking, so this is something I invented for him to try out. It's so easy to make because all it involves is throwing a few things into the pot and leaving it in the oven for a while. In Andy's case he'll go to a football match while it's cooking so it's ready as soon as he gets home. You can serve it as a stew or in tortillas with crunchy salad and guacamole. The other great thing about it is that you can bulk it out with different types of roughly chopped root veg, or butternut squash, or even with different types of beans (try cannellini, flageolet or butter beans), and if you want a bit of heat, feel free to add a couple of crumbled dried chillies. PS Andy is a strapping lad currently looking for a wife if any of you can help – just look out for him out on the town in Saffron Walden at the weekend!

SERVES 4

olive oil

800g potatoes, peeled and chopped
   into 2.5cm dice

2 red onions, peeled and roughly
   chopped

2 carrots, peeled and roughly chopped

2 sticks of celery, trimmed and roughly
   chopped

2 sprigs of fresh rosemary, leaves picked

1 level teaspoon ground cumin

1 heaped tablespoon smoked paprika

1 orange

800g stewing steak, lamb or pork,
   cubed

1 x 400g jar or tin of chickpeas, drained

2 x 400g tins of quality plum tomatoes,
   chopped

4 tablespoons natural yoghurt

1 bunch of fresh coriander,
   leaves picked

First of all you need to preheat the oven, but the temperature will depend on how long you want to cook the stew for. If you want it ready in 3 hours, preheat it to 180°C/350°F/gas 4, but if you want to cook it for 6 hours, then you need the oven on at 140°C/275°F/gas 1.

Put a large casserole pan on the hob on a high heat, drizzle in 2 lugs of oil, then add the potatoes, onions, carrots, celery, rosemary, cumin, paprika, and orange zest and juice, and stir together. Cook for 1 minute, then mix again before adding the meat, the chickpeas and the tomatoes. Season lightly with sea salt and black pepper and pour over enough water to cover everything. Bring to the boil and put into the oven. You are now free to go out for a few hours (for the whole day if you want to!). Serve the stew in bowls with a dollop of yoghurt and a sprinkle of coriander leaves.

CALORIES	FAT	SAT FAT	PROTEIN	CARBS	SUGAR	SALT	FIBRE
696kcal	21.4g	5.2g	60.8g	68.6g	16.8g	1.2g	11.4g

MY FISHy FRIENDS

PLAICE
TURBOT
HALIBUT
COD
SARDINE
HADDOCK
WHITING
MACKEREL
SEA BREAM
SALMON
TROUT
MULLET
SWORDFISH

Some of the healthiest nations in the world consume a huge amount of fish. In Britain, though, I don't think we eat enough fish or do enough to promote it, especially when you consider that we live on an island. I think there are two major factors: the first is that people can often be too scared to have a go at cooking fish, and the second is that fish isn't sold fresh enough. When it comes to buying fish it's very simple: if it smells of the sea and looks shiny and beautiful, then you should want to buy it.

I really want to encourage you all to eat more oily fish as it's so good for you. My mate Jane Clarke, who's a fantastic nutritionist, was telling me that oily fish (like salmon, fresh tuna, herrings, kippers, mackerel and sardines) provide a rich source of a polyunsaturated oil called omega 3 fatty acids. These omega oils are crucial for keeping us healthy – they not only help to protect our hearts, but they also help to prevent strokes and some forms of cancer, as well as helping to relieve the symptoms of arthritis. Some research even suggests that omega 3 can improve kids' concentration, moods and behaviour. So, what's stopping you ... get down to the shops, buy some oily fish and serve it to the family this week! If you can eat a portion twice a week, even better. And please don't think that non-oily fish without the omega oils, such as plaice and haddock, are off the menu. They contain high levels of protein, vitamins and minerals, and are very good for you. So let's all eat fish!

In this chapter I've used the traybaking method several times because I've received so many letters and emails from people who've had success with this way of cooking. It's great because it means that your vegetables and fish cook at the same time and flavour each other.

If you don't feel confident about cooking fish, have a go at traybaking first. Then, if you find you're enjoying it and you want to do more, have a look at other books on the subject, such as *Fresh* by Mitchell Tonks, or any of Rick Stein's books.

LAKSA-STYLE SCALLOPS WITH SWEET CHILLI SAUCE

A laksa is a cross between a stew and a curry but it uses fragrant flavourings like ginger and lemongrass as opposed to heavy spices. Instead of scallops you can use cheaper fish like salmon or cod, sliced up – I'd suggest that you need about 400g. You can even use finely sliced chicken – just simmer it a little more slowly and for longer. This recipe really is open to any type of fish or budget – my version is great with prawns in the base and scallops on the top.

SERVES 4

300g peeled prawns, roughly chopped
3 limes
2 tablespoons fish sauce
2–3 fresh red chillies, deseeded
3 cloves of garlic
5cm piece of ginger, peeled
1 bunch of fresh coriander, leaves
   picked, stalks reserved
1 tablespoon groundnut oil

1 small handful of kaffir lime leaves
olive oil
1 teaspoon tamarind paste
2 x 400g tins of light coconut milk
140ml quality chicken stock
12 scallops, trimmed
200g noodles
optional: 4 spring onions, finely sliced,
   or 1 punnet of cress, chopped

Put the prawns into a bowl and finely grate over the lime zest. Squeeze over the juice of 2 of the limes and add the fish sauce. Mix well, and leave to marinate for 10 minutes. In a pestle and mortar or a food processor, pound or blitz the chillies, garlic, ginger, coriander stalks, groundnut oil and lime leaves until you have a paste. Drizzle 2 tablespoons of olive oil into a large casserole or wok, with the paste, stirring quickly. Cook for 1 minute before adding the prawns and juices from the bowl. Allow to cook for another minute, stirring, then add the tamarind paste, coconut milk and chicken stock. Turn the heat down and simmer slowly for 15 minutes. Taste – you may need to add sea salt and black pepper or more fish sauce, and just enough lime juice to give it a good twang, as Asian food should be hot, salty, sweet and sour.

Lightly score the scallops with a criss-cross pattern on one side so that they will open out as they cook. Drizzle a little olive oil into a large non-stick frying pan, add the lightly seasoned scallops to the pan and cook for 2 minutes on each side, or until golden. Cook the noodles in a pan of boiling salted water according to the packet instructions.

Remove the scallops from the heat. Drain the noodles and divide between serving bowls, spooning the laksa stew over the top. Sprinkle with the coriander leaves – or you can try some finely sliced spring onions or some cress to give a bit of a crunch – then dot the scallops on top. Lovely served with a dollop of sweet chilli jam, which you can buy just about everywhere these days.

CALORIES	FAT	SAT FAT	PROTEIN	CARBS	SUGAR	SALT	FIBRE
561kcal	25.5g	12.6g	36.5g	48.5g	6.8g	2.3g	1.8g

SUMMER TRAYBAKED SALMON

This is one of those great dishes that you can make your own by using whatever vegetables are in season – it's particularly nice with broad beans, asparagus or cherry tomatoes. The fish doesn't take long to cook, so you can blanch the veg accordingly, then finish them off in the tray with the fish. It makes life a lot easier if you're cooking for the family or a large group of friends.

SERVES 4
800g new potatoes
1 large handful of runner beans, sliced into 5cm pieces
1 large handful of green beans, tops trimmed
optional: 1 large handful of yellow French beans, tops trimmed
2 handfuls of podded fresh peas
50g unsalted butter
olive oil
2 lemons
1 bunch of fresh basil
1 handful of fresh fennel tops or dill
4 x 200g salmon fillets, skin on, scaled, pin-boned

Preheat the oven to 230°C/450°F/gas 8. Cook the potatoes in a large pan of boiling salted water for 10 to 12 minutes, or until nearly tender. Add all the beans to the pan and cook for another 4 minutes, then drain. Tip everything into an appropriately sized roasting tray and add the peas, the butter, a little drizzle of oil and the zest and juice of the lemons. Season lightly with sea salt and black pepper and toss together while still warm so the flavours are absorbed.

Chop half the herbs and add to the tray. Score the salmon fillets lightly on the skin side. Rub each fillet with salt, pepper and a little oil, and stuff the scores with the remaining herbs. Roast for 10 to 15 minutes, or until the salmon is just cooked (don't overcook it) and the veggies are soft. Serve at the table, giving everyone some veggies and potatoes, a nice piece of salmon and some of the lovely cooking juices from the bottom of the tray which are like a ready-made sauce. Great with some garlicky yoghurt or mayonnaise.

CALORIES	FAT	SAT FAT	PROTEIN	CARBS	SUGAR	SALT	FIBRE
699kcal	42.3g	12.4g	46g	35.7g	4.8g	0.7g	5.9g

ITALIAN-STYLE UPSIDE-DOWN FISH PIE

This was one of the big revelations of last year for me. Don't think you're going to get your traditional fish pie – with this you'll get something more stylish and subtle. And the great thing about it is that it can be flexible on the budget – you can make it cheaply with things like mussels and haddock, or you can spend a bit more on things like lobster. As long as the fish is sliced around the same thickness it really doesn't matter what you use. But what you will have to do is ask your fishmonger to fillet all the fish for you, and it will also have to be pin-boned. If using clams and mussels, make sure they are cleaned and debearded. Throw away any that are open and after cooking chuck away any that remain closed.

SERVES 4

150g polenta
100g freshly grated Parmesan cheese
100g unsalted butter
olive oil
200g mixed mushrooms, left whole or
    torn up
2 cloves of garlic, peeled and
    finely chopped
500g baby spinach
1 whole nutmeg, for grating
2 lemons

800g mixed seafood, such as red mullet,
    monkfish, bream (filleted, scaled,
    pin-boned, sliced), prawns (peeled
    and deveined), mussels (debearded)
    – see intro
2 handfuls of red or yellow cherry
    tomatoes, halved
1 red chilli, deseeded and finely
    chopped
1 bunch of fresh thyme, leaves picked

In a high-sided, heavy-bottomed pan, cook the polenta according to the packet instructions – it will make a very soft 'blup blup blup' noise! Add the Parmesan and the butter, and season to taste with sea salt and black pepper, otherwise it will be too bland. Once done, put a lid on top and keep warm, until needed.

Preheat the oven to 230°C/450°F/gas 8. Drizzle a little oil into a large ovenproof frying pan or roasting tray on a medium heat, then add the mushrooms and garlic. Fry for 2 or 3 minutes, then add the spinach. Continue to cook until the spinach wilts and goes dark green and any liquid has cooked away. Grate over the nutmeg and season very carefully to taste with salt, pepper and a tiny squeeze of lemon juice. At this point you can turn the heat off, shake the pan so the mushrooms lie flat, and pour the wet polenta over the top to give you a nice layer.

Place the seafood, tomatoes, 2 tablespoons of oil and the zest and juice of the lemons into a bowl. Season with salt and pepper, add the chilli and thyme, then toss together. Sprinkle over the top of the polenta, pouring over any juices. Cook in the oven for 10 to 15 minutes (the fish shouldn't need any longer than this), then take straight to the table and serve.

CALORIES	FAT	SAT FAT	PROTEIN	CARBS	SUGAR	SALT	FIBRE
626kcal	35.6g	19g	43.3g	33.9g	2.8g	1.6g	4g

SPICED FRIED FISH WITH A SPEEDY TARTARE SAUCE

I've had lots of fun serving this as an appetizer at dinner parties, or even for a starter at the restaurant. This way you don't need to have a massive pot and loads of oil heating up. And you can get it all done in one or two batches. You can pretty much deep-fry any fish, and they'll all cook together very happily provided they're sliced to the same thickness or size. All you need to do is make sure that the fish have been scaled, filleted and pin-boned. In the case of prawns you will need to peel, devein and butterfly them, and if you're using squid, it should be skinned and gutted. Ask your fishmonger to give you a selection of fish that will take the same length of time to cook – I particularly love using squid, sole, bass, bream, prawns and mullet. Once you've been to the fishmonger's, let's be honest, most of the work's done for you, so all your love and attention can go on the cooking, which is the key here.

SERVES 4

sunflower oil
1 small piece of potato
1 handful of fennel seeds
3 dried red chillies
75g plain flour
800g mixed seafood (filleted, scaled, pin-boned) – see intro

TARTARE SAUCE

4 heaped tablespoons mayonnaise
1 handful of baby capers, finely chopped
1 handful of gherkins, finely chopped
zest and juice of 1 lemon
1 splash of white wine vinegar

Make the tartare sauce by mixing all the ingredients together in a bowl. Season to taste with sea salt and black pepper and put to one side. Now get yourself a large casserole pan with reasonably high sides. I wouldn't recommend a wok for this recipe, as they're not all that stable or safe for deep-frying. Fill the pan with 4cm of sunflower oil and place a small piece of potato in it. Turn the heat on – by the time the potato is golden you'll know you're at the right frying temperature. It normally takes about 10 minutes to heat up, but as usual you need to be around and be vigilant, so don't leave the pan unattended. If the oil starts to smoke it is too hot, so turn it down.

Meanwhile, in a coffee grinder or a pestle and mortar, whiz or bash the fennel seeds and chillies to a powder, then mix well with the flour. Now, if you've got a big pan, you may be able to do all the fish at the same time, but if not, then you need to cook them in two batches. Toss all the fish in the spiced flour and gently shake off any excess. Lower the fish carefully into the oil, one piece at a time to avoid splashing, making sure the heat is on full whack as the fish will reduce the temperature of the oil and you need it as hot as possible. Using a slotted spoon, slowly move the fish around. Cook for 2 minutes, or until golden and crisp, then remove to kitchen paper to drain. Serve at the table on a platter, a plate or even some newspaper! Give it a good sprinkling of salt and serve with the tartare sauce. Simple but great.

CALORIES	FAT	SAT FAT	PROTEIN	CARBS	SUGAR	SALT	FIBRE
586kcal	42.3g	5.1g	37.6g	16.7g	1g	2.1g	1.3g

GRILLED & TRAYBAKED RATATOUILLE
WITH WHITE FISH

This recipe for delicate white fish baked on top of a sweet and easy ratatouille is just lovely. Again, in the typical traybaked way, the ratatouille benefits from being flavoured by the fish juices and at the same time it will steam its flavour into the fish. Ratatouille is a kind of vegetable stew which originates from Nice in the south of France. I've made my own version of this dish using a slightly different technique. I think the end result looks great and tastes fantastic, so I hope you enjoy it.

SERVES 4

3 red peppers
1 bulb of fennel, trimmed
1 red onion, peeled
olive oil
3 firm aubergines
4 firm green courgettes, trimmed and
    chopped into 1cm pieces
2 cloves of garlic, peeled and chopped
1 bunch of fresh basil, leaves picked,
    stalks finely chopped
2 handfuls of black and green
    olives, stone in

2 x 400g tins of quality plum
    tomatoes, chopped
2 fresh bay leaves
1 tablespoon red wine vinegar
800g white fish, such as lemon or Dover
    sole, sea bass, haddock or monkfish
    (filleted, scaled, pin-boned), cut into
    similar-sized pieces – or even squid
    and prawns
½ a lemon

Preheat the oven to 190°C/375°F/gas 5. Using a pair of tongs, hold the peppers over a naked flame on a gas hob or place on a barbecue. Once blackened, put the peppers into a large sandwich bag and secure – this will allow them to steam – leave for 30 minutes before peeling and deseeding. Chop the fennel and onion into rough 1cm pieces and put into a large casserole pan or roasting tray with a little oil. Toss together, then cook over a medium heat while you prepare the rest of the vegetables. Quarter the aubergines lengthways, then remove the fluffy core. Chop into 1cm pieces, leaving the skin on. When the fennel and onion have had 5 or 6 minutes and have softened nicely, remove to a plate. Turn the heat up to full whack, pour in a small amount of oil, and add the aubergines, courgettes, garlic and basil stalks. Cook for 6 minutes, stirring regularly to mix everything together. Squash the olives and remove the stones. Add the tomatoes to the vegetables, along with the fennel and onion, olives, bay leaves and red wine vinegar. Season lightly with sea salt and black pepper and give it a good stir. Pop the tray into the oven for 40 minutes to allow the sauce to thicken – you can loosely cover the tray with tin foil or wet greaseproof paper.

Dress the fish with a little oil, a squeeze of lemon juice and some salt and pepper. Remove the ratatouille from the oven, season to taste, then add all the basil leaves, either whole or torn, and give it a good stir. Lay the fish over the top and pop back in the oven. If the fish pieces are reasonably thin, they should only need 5 minutes, but give them slightly longer if you prefer. Delicious served with crusty bread and a good glass of wine.

CALORIES	FAT	SAT FAT	PROTEIN	CARBS	SUGAR	SALT	FIBRE
418kcal	12.8g	2.5g	46.2g	32.5g	23.9g	1.8g	7.9g

TRAYBAKED SEA BASS WITH CRISPY ROASTED ASPARAGUS BUNDLES WRAPPED IN BACON

This is another of my favourite traybaked dishes. I like to serve it in the tray at the table, so that people can help themselves to the bits that they like best. It's a really great way to cook for your family, and your bambinos should love it. What you're going to get from this is some tremendous veg, some wonderfully cooked fish, some crispy smoky bacon and a lovely wine sauce at the bottom of the tray. If you want to have some new potatoes on the side, or a green salad, feel free.

SERVES 4
4 x 225g thin sea bass fillets, scaled, pin-boned, trimmed
olive oil
2½ lemons
1 handful of runner beans, tops trimmed
1 handful of green or yellow French beans, tops trimmed
1 handful of white or green asparagus, trimmed
1 bunch of fresh mint
8 rashers of smoked streaky bacon
2 wineglasses of Chardonnay
85g unsalted butter, cubed

Preheat the oven to full whack (240°C/475°F/gas 9). Score the sea bass fillets, then get yourself a large sandwich bag or dish. Put the fillets into your chosen bag or dish with a little swig of oil. Finally grate in the zest of 2 lemons and squeeze in the juice, then leave to marinate for 10 minutes. Parboil all the beans and asparagus for 2 to 3 minutes, then drain.

Meanwhile, smash up most of the mint in a pestle and mortar (or use a metal bowl with a rolling pin) until you have a pulp. Add a little oil to loosen, and the juice from the remaining lemon half. Tip the drained beans and asparagus into a large roasting tray and toss with the mint oil. Divide the beans and asparagus into bundles and wrap them snugly with some strips of bacon to secure. Put these bundles into the roasting tray, then remove the fish fillets from the bag and intermingle them with the bundles. Pour the wine into the tray, season with sea salt and black pepper and cook for 10 minutes, or until the fish and bacon are both golden. Remove from the oven, add the cubes of butter, and allow to rest for a few minutes. Give the tray a shake, then take to the table. Serve the fish drizzled with some of the white wine sauce from the tray and sprinkled with the rest of the mint.

CALORIES	FAT	SAT FAT	PROTEIN	CARBS	SUGAR	SALT	FIBRE
691kcal	46g	17.7g	49.9g	6.2g	4.8g	1.5g	2.8g

TASTY FISH BAKE

Although I've eaten dishes similar to this in the past, this particular fish bake was brought to my attention recently by one of my students. It's essentially some slow-cooked 'jammified' sweet onions and fennel, layered with lovely, flaky fish, crunchy potatoes and breadcrumbs with a little cream and cheese, then baked in the oven. When you eat it, make sure to get a bit of every layer on your fork! The dish makes wonderful use of trout (as I've used here), sardines, salmon or mackerel – any fish really, but oily ones are great to use, especially for kids. Try to get hold of the freshest fish you can, and ask your fishmonger to prepare it and get rid of the bones for you.

SERVES 4
400g potatoes, finely sliced
olive oil
1 clove of garlic, peeled and chopped
1 onion, peeled and sliced
1 bulb of fennel, trimmed and sliced
1 teaspoon fennel seeds
4 medium or 8 small fillets of trout, skin on, scaled, pin-boned
250ml single cream
2 handfuls of freshly grated Parmesan cheese, plus extra for sprinkling
2 anchovy fillets, in oil, chopped
2 handfuls of fresh breadcrumbs
2 lemons, cut into wedges

Preheat the oven to 200°C/400°F/gas 6. Parboil the sliced potatoes in boiling salted water for a few minutes, or until softened, then drain. Place a 20cm casserole pan on a low heat, pour in 4 tablespoons of oil, then add the garlic, onion, fennel and fennel seeds, and cook slowly for 10 minutes with the lid on, stirring occasionally.

Take the pan off the heat. Lay the trout fillets skin-side up over the onion and fennel. Mix the cream, Parmesan and anchovies, season with sea salt and black pepper, and pour over the fish. Toss the potato slices in a little olive oil, salt and pepper and layer these over the top. Place in the oven for 20 minutes, or until golden and cooked through, sprinkling with the breadcrumbs and a little grated Parmesan 5 minutes before the end. Serve with lemon wedges, a green salad and cold beers!

CALORIES	FAT	SAT FAT	PROTEIN	CARBS	SUGAR	SALT	FIBRE
601kcal	36.4g	13.1g	36.5g	34.8g	5.6g	2.1g	5.7g

SKATE SIMMERED IN A SWEET TOMATO SAUCE

I got the idea for this skate dish when I was in Sicily and was served a large loin of tuna (the length of my arm!) poached in a fragrant tomato sauce. The results were fantastic – the fish and sauce had each flavoured the other and both had become the better for it. A bit like a good marriage! As large pieces of fresh tuna are reasonably hard to get hold of, I tried it with skate. The results were just as good, as skate has a fantastic meaty texture too, so feel free to use either fish in this recipe.

SERVES 4

4 x 250g skate or ray wings, trimmed
1 red onion, peeled and
    finely chopped
4 cloves of garlic, peeled and
    finely chopped
1 teaspoon coriander seeds, bashed
olive oil

3 x 400g tins of quality plum tomatoes,
    finely chopped or puréed
2 lemons
12 anchovy fillets, in oil, halved
a few sprigs of fresh rosemary,
    leaves picked

Preheat the oven to 180°C/350°F/gas 4. Find yourself a large casserole pan or deep roasting tray that will fit all the skate wings in (the skate needs to be totally covered by the sauce, so make sure it fits in nice and snugly). In this pan or tray, slowly fry the onion, garlic and coriander seeds in 2 lugs of oil until softened. Add the tomatoes, finely grate in the lemon zest and squeeze in the juice and season lightly with sea salt and black pepper, then bring to a simmer.

Meanwhile, using the tip of a small, sharp knife, make small incisions in the fatter central part of the fish. Push half an anchovy fillet into each incision, then spike with a small piece of rosemary. Do this three times on both sides of each fish. Carefully submerge the fish in the tomato sauce, making sure that every part is covered. Put the pan or tray into the oven and cook for 15 minutes, depending on how thick the wings are (if the flesh pulls off the bone, you know it's cooked beautifully). Correct the seasoning and take to the table straight away. Serve it as is, with just the sauce for company, or with things like mashed potato or polenta, salad or garden greens. Toss any leftovers with pasta. My favourite way is just with some ciabatta to mop up the tomato sauce.

CALORIES	FAT	SAT FAT	PROTEIN	CARBS	SUGAR	SALT	FIBRE
304kcal	7.5g	0.9g	45g	15.8g	14.2g	2.4g	3.9g

PAN-COOKED GIANT PRAWNS
WITH MANGETOUT, PEAS & BUTTER BEANS

This recipe was great fun to make up. I was shopping at Borough Market and decided to buy some fantastic giant prawns, then a jar of butter beans and a handful of mangetout and peas. Next I bought a paella pan and went along to see my friend Maria, who works at the Borough Market Café. She let me use one of the rings on her gas hob and I got cooking … Don't be put off by thinking that large prawns are expensive, because they're actually quite good value. However, this recipe works with all sorts of different prawns.

SERVES 4
olive oil
12 large raw king prawns, peeled, deveined, butterflied
1–2 fresh red chillies, finely sliced
1 bunch of spring onions, trimmed and finely sliced
4 large handfuls of mangetout
2 large handfuls of fresh podded peas
2 x 400g tins of butter or cannellini beans
500g ripe tomatoes, chopped
1 big bunch of fresh flat-leaf parsley, leaves picked and finely chopped
1–2 lemons

Get yourself a large paella or casserole pan, wok or sturdy roasting tin. Put it on the hob and get it nice and hot, then pour in 3 or 4 tablespoons of oil and add the prawns. Allow them to colour on one side, then turn them over, sprinkling them first with the chilli and spring onions. Add the mangetout and peas to the pan, give it a shake, then add a splash of water, put a lid (or some tin foil) on top and let everything steam for 1 minute.

Remove the lid (or tin foil), then add the butter beans and tomatoes. Give it all a stir, simmer for 2 minutes, or until softened, then correct the seasoning. Throw in the parsley and squeeze over lemon juice, to taste. Serve in the middle of the table – wonderful with rice, couscous or grilled bread.

CALORIES	FAT	SAT FAT	PROTEIN	CARBS	SUGAR	SALT	FIBRE
230kcal	10.9g	1.7g	18.7g	15g	5.9g	0.9g	4.9g

OMEGA 3 & COUSCOUS

Silly name, but what a great dish! Omega 3 refers to all the lovely goodness that you get from oily fish like red mullet, sardines and fresh anchovies, so do feel free to use any one of these, or a mixture of them. This is also great served with linguine instead of couscous.

SERVES 4

500g red mullet, scaled, filleted,
    pin-boned
olive oil
2 red onions, peeled and finely
    chopped
1 bulb of fennel, herby tops
    reserved, bulb finely chopped
1 fresh red chilli, finely chopped
1 teaspoon fennel seeds

1 fresh bay leaf
300g couscous
500g ripe tomatoes
2 anchovy fillets, in oil, chopped
2 lemons
8 tablespoons natural yoghurt
½ a bunch of fresh mint, leaves
    picked and torn

First of all, lay the fish out in one layer on a clean worktop to give you an idea of how much you're dealing with. Next get yourself a pan with a lid – ideally one that's the right size for the fish to be spread out in one layer, (this is so that it can all cook at the same time). Put the pan on the heat, drizzle in 4 or 5 tablespoons of oil, and slowly fry the onions, fennel, chilli, fennel seeds and bay with the lid on for 10 minutes, or until softened.

Put the couscous in a bowl, then just cover with boiling salted water. Pop a plate on top and leave to fluff up. When the onions are sweet and soft, add the tomatoes and anchovies, stir together and carefully season to taste with sea salt and black pepper. Shake the pan so that the onions and tomatoes cover the bottom evenly. Dress the couscous lightly with oil and the juice and zest of one of the lemons. Sprinkle the couscous over the top of the onions and tomatoes in one even layer, then place the fish over the top of that and finish off with a drizzle of oil. Place the lid on top and simmer slowly on the hob for 12 minutes, or until beautifully cooked. Meanwhile, season the yoghurt with salt, pepper and the remaining lemon juice. Sprinkle the reserved fennel tops and mint over the fish, then serve in the middle of the table with the yoghurt and let everyone help themselves.

CALORIES	FAT	SAT FAT	PROTEIN	CARBS	SUGAR	SALT	FIBRE
536kcal	24.1g	3.6g	33.3g	49.3g	10.4g	1.1g	4.3g

les junior's fish stall at borough market –
just gets better every year. well done, mate.

THE NICEST TRAYBAKED LEMON SOLE

This recipe can be applied to any size of flat fish. Out of all the soles, lemon sole is the most widely available and generally good value for money. This method of cooking is really simple. Not only does it give you a really clean-tasting fish, but also a juicy, chunky sauce with the added benefit of all the natural juices. It's quick and easy and I would recommend serving in the tray at the table with new potatoes, salad and some crisp white wine.

SERVES 4
4 whole lemon sole
2 handfuls of red and yellow cherry tomatoes, halved
4 cloves of garlic, peeled and finely sliced
1 bunch of fresh oregano or basil, leaves picked
1 bunch of spring onions, trimmed and finely sliced
1 tablespoon balsamic vinegar
2 lemons
olive oil
1 handful of black olives, stone in
1 bunch of fresh flat-leaf parsley, leaves picked and finely chopped

With a sharp knife, score across each fish down to the bone at 2.5cm intervals on both sides – this allows flavour to penetrate and lets the juices come out.

Preheat the oven to 200°C/400°F/gas 6. To a bowl, add the tomatoes, garlic, oregano or basil, spring onions, balsamic, and a pinch of sea salt and black pepper. Finely grate in the zest of 1 lemon and squeeze in the juice. Loosen with 2 tablespoons of oil, mix well, then spread over the bottom of a large roasting tray (or two smaller trays). Place the fish on top – top to tail.

Squash the olives and remove the stones, then roughly chop and add to the bowl the tomatoes were in, along with the parsley. Finely grate in the zest from the remaining lemon and squeeze in the juice. Loosen with a little oil and divide this mixture between the fish, placing an equal amount on the centre of each. Cook in the oven for 12 to 15 minutes, depending on the size of the fish. To check whether they're done, take the tip of a knife and push it into the thickest part – the flesh should easily pull away from the bone.

Once cooked, allow the fish to rest for 3 or 4 minutes while you get your guests round the table, serve them some wine and dress the salad. Divide the fish up at the table, making sure that everyone gets some tomatoes and juice spooned over the top. Lovely!

CALORIES	FAT	SAT FAT	PROTEIN	CARBS	SUGAR	SALT	FIBRE
366kcal	13.6g	3.1g	55.5g	5.2g	3.5g	1.5g	1.5g

CONCERTINA SQUID

This is a really cool way of prepping squid. It makes the squid look great and allows it to take on flavours and seasoning in a really interesting way. You can see from the picture why I've called it 'concertina squid' as it reminds me of a concertina, or accordion, when it opens out. It can be served hot or cold as a main dish or a salad. Simple but totally scrumptious.

SERVES 4

800g new potatoes
½ a bunch of fresh mint, leaves picked and chopped, stalks tied together
2 knobs of unsalted butter
olive oil
1kg medium squid, gutted, cleaned
1 red onion, peeled and finely sliced

1 bunch of fresh flat-leaf parsley, leaves picked and roughly chopped, stalks finely chopped
1 tablespoon ground white pepper
2 cloves of garlic, peeled and finely grated or chopped
1–2 fresh red chillies, deseeded and finely sliced
2 lemons

Cook the new potatoes in boiling salted water with the mint stalks for 20 to 25 minutes, or until slightly overcooked, then drain and steam dry while you heat up a large frying pan. Put a knob of butter and 2 tablespoons of oil into the pan, add the potatoes and, using a pair of tongs or a spoon, lightly crush them and toss them around for 5 minutes, or until lightly golden. While these are cooking, you are going to prepare your squid – I've given you some step-by-step photographs to help you out (see pages 278–9).

Take a squid and place a large cook's or palette knife into the tube. Using another cook's knife, slice the squid along its length at 1cm intervals. As the second knife cuts down on to the first, a fantastic effect is achieved whereby the squid retains its overall shape but also opens up a bit like a concertina. Repeat with the remaining squid, reserving the tentacles.

Once the potatoes are golden, add the onion and parsley stalks and give the pan a good shake. Toss the scored squid and the tentacles in a bowl with the white pepper and a tiny pinch of sea salt. When the onions are golden, turn them and the potatoes out on to a plate, put the pan back on the heat, add a little oil and fry the squid for 2 minutes on each side. Once nicely golden, add the remaining butter, garlic, chilli and parsley leaves. Give the squid a really good shake to take on all the beautiful flavours, then put the potatoes and onions back into the pan. Toss together, then season to taste. Squeeze over the lemon juice – this will give it all a nice twang – and divide between plates, sprinkled with the mint leaves.

CALORIES	FAT	SAT FAT	PROTEIN	CARBS	SUGAR	SALT	FIBRE
501kcal	20.3g	7.4g	43.2g	37g	5.3g	1g	4.8g

1. insert your chopper
inside the squid

2. slice through the top of the squid on to the knife. hey presto!

SOUTH AMERICAN FISHCAKES

I learnt this recipe from my friend Santos, who comes from Brazil, where they make little fritters of this recipe and deep-fry them – more like glorified canapés than fishcakes really. I've adapted his recipe slightly to make actual fishcakes – probably the nicest I've tasted! In Brazil they're called 'bolinho de bacalhau' and are made with salt cod, which is a wonderful fish to use if you can get hold of it. However, for this recipe I've simply used flaked white fish. Quite a few cookbooks have recipes for fishcakes these days, but they all seem to be Thai-influenced, with overly clever and complicated seasonings or dips. The nice thing about this one is that you can taste the potatoes and fish alongside the heat of the chilli and the zing of the lemons and limes. It works a treat.

PS My sister wanted to know if these fishcakes could be pan-fried instead of deep-fried. The answer is yes, they can be, but you will need to control the temperature. Fishcakes that are 2cm thick will need roughly 2 minutes 30 seconds on each side.

MAKES LOTS!

1kg haddock fillets, skin on, scaled, pin-boned
150ml milk
2 fresh bay leaves
1kg potatoes, peeled and diced
2 lemons, plus extra to serve
2 limes
1 big bunch of fresh flat-leaf parsley, leaves picked and finely chopped

½ a bunch of fresh mint, leaves picked and finely chopped
1 teaspoon fennel seeds, bashed
2 large eggs
1 fresh red chilli, finely chopped
100g plain flour
sunflower oil, for frying

Preheat the oven to 190°C/375°F/gas 5. Place the haddock in a roasting tray with the milk and bay, cover with tin foil and cook for 15 minutes. Meanwhile, cook the potatoes in boiling salted water for 15 minutes, or until tender, then drain and steam dry. Return to a low heat and mash.

Flake the cooked fish into a large bowl, discarding the skin. Finely grate in the lemon and lime zest, then add the mashed potato, parsley, mint, fennel seeds, eggs and chilli. Season with sea salt and black pepper, then mix well. Flour a clean work surface, then take 1 tablespoon of the mix in your hands with a little flour and pat it into a flattened circle, rolling it in the flour. Rough and ready is good, so don't worry about having them all exactly the same!

Pour sunflower oil into a sturdy pan and heat it to 190°C. Carefully lower the fishcakes in one by one, so you don't get splashed. Cook for 5 minutes, or until golden and crispy. Drain on kitchen paper, sprinkle with salt and serve on a large plate with lots of lemon halves for squeezing over.

CALORIES	FAT	SAT FAT	PROTEIN	CARBS	SUGAR	SALT	FIBRE
219kcal	13.4g	1.8g	12.2g	13.6g	0.8g	0.3g	0.9g

THESE VALUES ARE BASED ON MAKING 20 FISHCAKES

For all of you who like desserts, there's no major theme for this chapter apart from it's a great collection of really solid recipes that are just perfect for making at home. I've used fruit in most of the recipes, as I think it's always a treat when you're working with rich desserts or sugar. I've also included a few of the great British classics like jam roly poly, sticky toffee pudding or a lovely Bakewell tart, and you must try the scented English creams – perfect for a summer's day! The tarts in particular are great with an afternoon cup of tea. Mmmmm! Quite a lot of people think they shouldn't eat desserts, but I don't think there's anything wrong with a little – just don't eat the whole lot!

BAKED PEARS WITH WINE & SCRUMPTIOUS WALNUT CREAM

When I worked in France I would visit a lovely little bakery once a week to buy a tart filled with a really amazing walnut cream, with poached glazed pears on top. It was such a joy to eat that I wanted to give you a recipe based on these flavours – the combination is fantastic. At Christmas time it's nice to use chestnuts instead of walnuts, or you could even bash up or grate some quality chocolate to sprinkle over the pears as well.

SERVES 4
1 vanilla pod
4 seasonal pears, peeled
125g dark muscovado sugar, plus a little extra
2 large wineglasses of red or white wine
2 oranges
200g shelled unsalted walnuts
200g mascarpone cheese

Preheat the oven to 220ºC/425ºF/gas 7. Score the vanilla pod lengthways and scrape out the seeds. Put the pears into a tight-fitting ovenproof pan, add the sugar, wine, vanilla pod and seeds, and the peel and juice of 1 orange and bring to the boil. Sprinkle over half the walnuts, then bake for 20 to 30 minutes, depending on the ripeness, or until the pears are tender but still holding their shape. Baste the pears occasionally as they cook to give them a nice glaze. Once cooked, allow to cool while you toast the remaining walnuts for 5 minutes – make sure you keep an eye on them as they can quickly go from golden to black very quickly and you don't want burnt walnuts!

Remove the vanilla pod from the syrup. When the walnuts are done, either whiz them in a food processor or bash to a paste in a pestle and mortar. Whip up the mascarpone with the walnut paste, finely grate in the zest of the other orange and squeeze in the juice, then add just enough sugar to sweeten. Serve the cream with the pears, nuts, orange peel and some cooking syrup.

CALORIES	FAT	SAT FAT	PROTEIN	CARBS	SUGAR	SALT	FIBRE
853kcal	56.7g	18.5g	10.5g	55.4g	54.9g	0.2g	4.7g

SWEET VANILLA RISOTTO
WITH POACHED PEACHES & CHOCOLATE

People in Britain have always had a bit of a soft spot in their hearts for rice pudding. However, the convenience and relative quality of tinned Ambrosia rice pudding has stopped a lot of people cooking the real thing. I thought it would be good to get you making this lovely old British dessert, but with a northern Italian twist – in the style of a risotto. Pudding rice and risotto rice are both plump, short-grain and starchy, so I thought it would be a good test to see if risotto rice would make great rice pudding – and it did. It has to be one of the best rice puddings I've ever made! It's lovely served with the peaches, but you could also use apricots, strawberries or rhubarb.

SERVES 8

6 ripe peaches	300g risotto rice
6 tablespoons caster sugar	1 wineglass of white wine
½ a cinnamon stick	1 litre whole milk
1 orange	100g quality white chocolate, grated
45g unsalted butter	100g quality dark chocolate (70%)
2 vanilla pods	1 bunch of fresh mint, leaves picked

Halve the peaches, leaving the stones in – they will come away easily after cooking. Put them into a small pan with 4 tablespoons of the sugar and the cinnamon stick, then finely grate in the orange zest and squeeze in the juice. Put the lid on and simmer slowly for 10 to 15 minutes, or until the peach skin and stones can be easily removed. You don't want to cook them to a pulp – they should be soft but still holding their shape. Remove from the heat and put to one side.

In a large heavy-bottomed pan, slowly melt two-thirds of the butter. Score the vanilla pods lengthways and scrape out the seeds, then put into the pan. Continue to cook for 1 minute before adding the rice with the remaining sugar. Turn the heat up to medium, stir the rice, and add the wine, continuing to stir until it has almost cooked away. Now add the milk little by little. Keep the rice on a slow but constant simmer for about 16 or 17 minutes, stirring as often as you can. This will massage the starch out of the rice and give you a silky, oozy rice, much like a classic Italian risotto. Once cooked, the rice should be soft yet still holding its shape – add a little more milk or water just to adjust the consistency, if needed. Remove from the heat, add the white chocolate and the rest of the butter, then stir, cover and leave for a few minutes.

Remove and discard the cinnamon stick from the peaches, then take to the table with the block of dark chocolate, snapped into small pieces. Spoon the risotto on to plates, then push a couple of pieces of dark chocolate into the middle of each one. Just so you know, a perfect risotto should slowly creep and ooze to the side of your plate, so don't worry if it starts to spread out! Gently tear over the peaches, drizzle over with lovely juice and sprinkle over a few mint leaves. By the time you go to eat it, the dark chocolate will have melted. Joy joy joy!

CALORIES	FAT	SAT FAT	PROTEIN	CARBS	SUGAR	SALT	FIBRE
630kcal	24.9g	15.1g	12.6g	87.9g	44.4g	0.3g	2.9g

tranquillity now, but for how long . . . ?

TOFFEE APPLE TART

This is a fantastic dessert that I love to make for friends and family as they can't get enough of it. The combination of toffee and apples is a fairground classic but feel free to try it with pears, bananas, even strawberries – they're all absolutely delicious!

SERVES 8

SHORTCRUST PASTRY
optional: 1 vanilla pod
125g unsalted butter
100g icing sugar
250g plain flour
½ a lemon
2 large egg yolks
2 tablespoons cold milk

FILLING
2 x 397g tins of condensed milk or
    2 jars of Merchant Gourmet Dulce
    de Leche toffee
4 medium cooking apples
2 heaped tablespoons icing sugar

Put the unopened tins of condensed milk in a high-sided pan, covered with water. Bring to the boil, then reduce the heat and simmer for 3 hours with a lid on top. It's very important to remember to keep checking the pan, as you don't want it to boil dry – otherwise the tins will explode. It will give you the most amazing toffee. Put the tins to one side and allow to cool.

To make the pastry, score the vanilla pod lengthways (if using), and scape out the seeds (keep the pod for making vanilla sugar). Cream the butter, icing sugar and a small pinch of sea salt together, then rub in the flour. Add the vanilla seeds, finely grate in the lemon zest and add the egg yolks – you can do all this by hand or in a food processor. When the mixture looks like coarse breadcrumbs, add the cold milk (or use water). Pat and gently work the mixture together until you have a ball of dough, then flour it lightly and roll into a large sausage shape – don't work the pastry too much otherwise it will become elastic and chewy, not flaky and short as you want it to be. Wrap the dough in clingfilm and place in the fridge to rest for at least 1 hour. Remove it from the fridge, slice it up and line a 28cm loose-bottomed tart tin. Push the slices together, then tidy up the sides by trimming off any excess. Place the tart mould into the freezer for 1 hour.

Preheat the oven to 180°C/350°F/gas 4, then take the pastry case out of the freezer and bake for 15 minutes, or until lightly golden. Remove from the oven and allow to cool slightly. Peel and quarter the apples and remove the cores, then finely slice and toss in the icing sugar. Spread the caramel from both tins over the pastry case. Place the apples on top and pour any remaining juices over. Bake at the bottom of the oven for 40 minutes, to give you a crisp base and bubbling toffee over the apples. Serve with yoghurt or vanilla ice cream. Beautiful!

CALORIES	FAT	SAT FAT	PROTEIN	CARBS	SUGAR	SALT	FIBRE
666kcal	25.3g	14.6g	12.8g	103.4g	79.4g	0.5g	2.2g

CHOCOLATE CLAFOUTIS
WITH CARAMELIZED ORANGES

The nice thing about this recipe is that the fruit accompanying it can be varied – certain things work really well with chocolate, like oranges, clementines, apricots or cherries, so give them a try.

SERVES 8

5 oranges
100g quality dark chocolate (70%), broken up
80g unsalted butter
100g self-raising flour
100g ground almonds
100g sugar

2 large eggs
3 large egg yolks
180ml whole milk
100g quality white chocolate, broken up
optional: 500g crème fraîche or natural yoghurt

Preheat the oven to 200°C/400°F/gas 6. Finely grate the zest of 3 of the oranges, then carefully remove the outer peel and slice across into wheel-shaped pieces, just under 1cm thick. Place the dark chocolate in a small bowl and melt it over simmering water, stirring occasionally.

Butter the inside of a deep 20cm metal tin or earthenware dish. Sift the flour into a clean bowl, add the almonds, half the sugar, a pinch of sea salt, the eggs, yolks, orange zest and milk. Whisk up until smooth, then add the rest of the butter to the melting chocolate. Scrape all the melted chocolate and butter into the batter mix and pour into the tin. Poke little pieces of white chocolate into the batter, then bake in the oven for 16 to 20 minutes, or until firm around the edges but sticky and gooey in the middle. This doesn't mean it's undercooked ... it means it's perfect! So be careful not to overcook it or it will just be like a boring sponge.

While it's cooking, bring the other half of the sugar to the boil on a medium heat with 6 tablespoons of water until you have a golden caramel. Remove from the heat, squeeze in the juice from the remaining oranges and stir it in to loosen the caramel slightly. Arrange the orange slices nicely on a plate, pour over the caramel and serve with the chocolate clafoutis and a bowl of crème fraîche or yoghurt (if using). Delicious.

CALORIES	FAT	SAT FAT	PROTEIN	CARBS	SUGAR	SALT	FIBRE
637kcal	39.3g	17.3g	14.3g	59.2g	44.8g	0.7g	4.5g

THE ULTIMATE JAM ROLY POLY

This is something I had all the time for school dinner when I was at primary school. My mum also used to make it every now and again and it was always superb. The way the suet – which is completely underrated these days – gives the most fantastic, slightly chewy texture and it's all fluffy in the middle and slightly crisp on the outside ... I love it, really really nice. My version is based on the original golden oldie. I don't think it can be improved upon all that much, but what I think is quite nice is to bring some flavour into the batter and also to use some fruit. This works really well with the jam – it gives the whole thing a bit more texture and makes it more luxurious. Feel free to mix up the flavours – raspberry and strawberry together is one of my favourites.

SERVES 6

1 vanilla pod
225g self-raising flour, plus extra
   for dusting
1 heaped teaspoon baking powder
1 orange
150g beef suet, vegetarian suet
   or unsalted butter

150ml milk
175g quality strawberry and
   raspberry jam
3 large handfuls of strawberries
   and raspberries, sliced
1 large egg, beaten

Preheat the oven to 150°C/300°F/gas 2. Score the vanilla pod lengthways and scape out the seeds. Sift the flour into a large bowl, then add the baking powder, and finely grate in the orange zest. Add the vanilla seeds (keep the pod for making vanilla sugar) along with a pinch of sea salt and the suet or butter. Depending on the flour you're using, you may not need all the milk, so add it slowly until you have a soft but firm dough which isn't sticky. Leave to rest for 30 minutes, then lightly dust a clean surface with flour. Roll out the dough so it's about 30cm x 30cm. It doesn't have to be too perfect. Leaving a 2.5cm gap around the sides, spread the jam over the dough and scatter the strawberries on top. Brush the edges with some egg to help give it a nice seal.

The idea of the roly poly is that it's all rolled up so you get lovely layers of jam and sponge, but the jam from the early folds tends to get squeezed out, so I try to put a nice bit of jam in the first bit as I begin to roll it, then, as I fold the dough, pinch around it so that the jam gets trapped in and can't ooze out, then I continue to roll and pinch the ends to keep in all the jam.

When it's all rolled up, lay a piece of buttered greaseproof paper in front of it. Carefully roll the roly poly on to the paper and continue to roll it up so it is covered by the greaseproof, then get a double-layered sheet of tin foil and roll the roly poly in this as well, pinching the ends together. Place it on a rack above simmering water in a baking tray and cover it all with tin foil to allow it to steam in the oven for 2 hours. Top the tray up with boiling water every 30 minutes – simply peel back the foil to do this. This is one dessert that just has to be eaten with custard – nothing else will do!

CALORIES	FAT	SAT FAT	PROTEIN	CARBS	SUGAR	SALT	FIBRE
451kcal	23.6g	13.2g	6g	56.8g	23.8g	1.1g	2.4g

CHEAT'S DESSERT

This is a dessert which is absolutely great for getting you out of trouble at the last minute if you have friends descending on you for dinner. Brilliantly simple!

SERVES 4
4 ginger biscuits
4 blood oranges or clementines
4 scoops of vanilla ice cream

SYRUP (OPTIONAL)
optional: 50g caster sugar
optional: 2 blood oranges

Smash the ginger biscuits up into crumbs using a pestle and mortar, or place them in a clean tea towel and bash with a rolling pin. Put them into a dish. Peel and slice the blood oranges or clementines, making sure you remove any pips. Now all you have to do to serve is put a scoop of ice cream on each plate and either sprinkle with the ginger crumbs or serve a pile of crumbs under the ice cream, and top with some blood orange slices.

If you want to take this up a notch, bring the caster sugar to the boil on a medium heat with 6 tablespoons of water until you have a golden caramel. Remove from the heat, squeeze in the juice from the extra 2 oranges and stir it in to loosen the caramel slightly. Pour this over the sliced oranges so they marinate in the caramelized juices, before serving.

CALORIES	FAT	SAT FAT	PROTEIN	CARBS	SUGAR	SALT	FIBRE
147kcal	4.7g	2.6g	2.6g	25.1g	20.7g	0.2g	1.7g

MAPLE SYRUP & PECAN TART

Maple syrup and pecans are fantastic Canadian flavours. What I've done here is make a traditional English treacle tart, but with maple syrup and golden syrup and added nuts.

SERVES 8
1 x shortcrust pastry recipe (see page 292)
50g unsalted butter
300g maple syrup
3 tablespoons golden syrup
175g breadcrumbs, half fine, half coarse
2 Cox's apples, grated
5cm piece of ginger, peeled and finely grated
2 handfuls of shelled unsalted pecans
2 oranges
optional: crème fraîche or vanilla ice cream
optional: 1 handful of thyme flowers

First of all, make and chill the pastry, then line a 28cm loose-bottomed tart tin with it. Place in the freezer for 1 hour. Preheat the oven to 180°C/350°F/gas 4, then take the pastry case out of the freezer and bake for 15 minutes, or until lightly golden. Remove from the oven and allow to cool slightly. Heat the butter, maple syrup and golden syrup together in a pan, then mix in the breadcrumbs, apples, ginger and half the pecans. Finely grate in the orange zest and stir through. Spoon into the pastry case and sprinkle over the remaining pecans. Bake in the oven for 20 minutes, or until golden and cooked through. Lovely served with some crème fraîche or vanilla ice cream and sprinkled with thyme flowers.

CALORIES	FAT	SAT FAT	PROTEIN	CARBS	SUGAR	SALT	FIBRE
590kcal	26.3g	12.6g	7.1g	85.2g	48.7g	0.4g	2.7g

BAKEWELL TART

This is pretty easy because all you need to put it together is a pastry recipe and a frangipane recipe. Bakewell tart is a classic English tea cake which, if made with a bit of love and some quality jam, well deserves to be a dessert in its own right.

SERVES 12
1 x shortcrust pastry recipe (see page 292)

FRANGIPANE
350g blanched whole almonds
250g unsalted butter
300g caster sugar
3 large eggs
6 tablespoons quality strawberry jam
1 handful of blanched flaked almonds
optional: 500g crème fraîche or natural yoghurt

First of all, make and chill the pastry, then line a 28cm loose-bottomed tart tin with it. Place in the freezer for 1 hour. Preheat the oven to 180°C/350°F/gas 4, then take the pastry case out of the freezer and bake for 15 minutes, or until lightly golden. Remove from the oven and allow to cool slightly. Turn the oven down to 170°C/325°F/gas 3.

To make the frangipane, blitz the whole almonds in a food processor until you have a fine powder and put this into a bowl. Beat the butter and sugar together until light and creamy, then add to the almonds. Lightly beat the eggs and add to the mixture. Fold in until completely mixed and smooth, then place in the fridge to firm up slightly.

Spread the jam over the pastry case. Pour the chilled frangipane mixture on top, and sprinkle with some flaked almonds. Bake the tart for 40 minutes, or until the almond mixture has become firm and golden on the outside but is still soft in the middle. Allow to cool for about 30 minutes, then serve with crème fraîche or yoghurt.

CALORIES	FAT	SAT FAT	PROTEIN	CARBS	SUGAR	SALT	FIBRE
699kcal	46.2g	18.5g	11.4g	63.7g	46g	0.2g	0.9g

STICKY TOFFEE PUDDING

You're going to love this pudding – it has a rich, fantastic flavour and the sauce is amazing. Fresh Medjool dates are best to use, but dried ones work well, too.

SERVES 8

225g fresh dates, stoned
1 teaspoon bicarbonate of soda
85g unsalted butter (at room temperature)
175g caster sugar
2 large eggs
175g self-raising flour
¼ teaspoon ground mixed spice
¼ teaspoon ground cinnamon
2 tablespoons Ovaltine
2 tablespoons natural yoghurt

TOFFEE SAUCE
100g unsalted butter
100g light muscovado sugar
140ml double cream

Preheat the oven to 180°C/350°F/gas 4. Put the dates in a bowl with the bicarbonate of soda and cover with 200ml of boiling water. Leave to stand for a couple of minutes to soften, then drain. Whiz in a food processor until you have a purée. Meanwhile, cream the butter and sugar together until pale, then add the eggs, flour, mixed spice, cinnamon and Ovaltine. Mix together well, then fold in the yoghurt and the puréed dates. Pour into a buttered, ovenproof dish and bake for 35 minutes, or until just cooked through.

While the pudding is cooking, make the toffee sauce by putting the butter, sugar and cream in a pan over a low heat until the sugar has dissolved and the sauce has thickened and darkened in colour. To serve, spoon out the pudding at the table and pour over the toffee sauce.

CALORIES	FAT	SAT FAT	PROTEIN	CARBS	SUGAR	SALT	FIBRE
570kcal	30.7g	17.9g	5.4g	73.3g	56.5g	0.7g	1.8g

SCENTED ENGLISH CREAMS

This is a kind of cross between an old-fashioned blancmange milk jelly and a pannacotta and was traditionally made in England as a variation on fruit jelly. It can be spiked with booze, flavoured with things like vanilla, lemon zest, cinnamon, coffee or orange and, like a good pannacotta, wants to be set so that it just holds together and isn't too bouncy or rubbery. I'm giving you a basic recipe to follow, with three different flavours, or scents, to add to it. Each of them uses 2½ leaves of gelatine and this is ideal if you want to make them the day before you need them. If making on the same day as eating, then you'll need an extra ½ a leaf.

MAKES 10

BASE RECIPE
600ml whole milk
200ml double cream
150g caster sugar
2½ leaves of gelatine

ORANGE & CARDAMOM CREAM
4 oranges
10 cardamom pods, roasted in a hot
   oven for 5 minutes then bashed up

BASIL CREAM
½ a bunch of fresh basil, leaves picked,
   stalks reserved and bashed up
optional: 10ml grappa

STRAWBERRY & STAR ANISE CREAM
200g quality strawberry jam
   (with strawberry bits!)
5 star anise

Put the milk, cream and sugar into a large pan and place on the heat. For the orange cream grate in all the orange zest and add the cardamom pods; for the basil cream add the basil stalks and grappa; for the strawberry cream just add the star anise. Bring to a gentle simmer, then remove from the heat and place to one side to infuse. While this is happening, soak the gelatine leaves in enough ice-cold water to cover and leave to soak for 10 minutes, or until they have softened.

Place the pan of milk back on the heat and bring to the boil. Whisk in the softened gelatine leaves until dissolved, then strain into a bowl. If making the orange cream, discard the orange zest and cardamom pods and pour the liquid into little moulds. For the basil cream bash up the basil leaves and add these to the pan. Give it a good stir, then strain the liquid, discarding the basil leaves and stalks, before pouring into moulds. If making the strawberry cream, remove from the heat and leave to cool to room temperature. Break the jam up with a fork until you have a nice loose consistency but with little bits of strawberry. Whisk the cooled milk liquid, then strain it, discarding the star anise, before pouring it into the jam. Stir together well and pour into moulds. Place in the fridge and leave to set for at least 4 hours, preferably overnight.

CALORIES	FAT	SAT FAT	PROTEIN	CARBS	SUGAR	SALT	FIBRE
197kcal	12.9g	8g	2.7g	18.9g	18.9g	0.1g	0g

THESE VALUES ARE BASED ON THE BASE RECIPE

KITCHENS THAT WORK

Loads of friends & people that I meet say, 'Oh, you always make cooking look so easy,' & add, 'I've only got a little kitchen,' as if that means that they can't do the same. The truth is that I don't have a big commercial kitchen that I produce it all from. To this day all my kitchens at home have been really small. The one that was featured on *The Naked Chef* was the most spacious, but it was cheaply made. However, a lot of commonsense to the layout made it work well. So here's a few points to help you get your kitchen organized which will give you more space & hopefully make you feel able to achieve more from it.

Most chefs & architects will agree that very rarely do you have the perfect shell to put a kitchen in – there will always be extraction problems or pillars or plumbing restrictions that make you compromise on the perfect design. If you're lucky enough to be designing a kitchen from scratch, here are some things to bear in mind. We all want a kitchen that looks good, but functionality is really important. Cupboards are always an issue because space is usually at a premium, especially as things like dishwashers are now built into what would have been extra cupboard space. Following on from here are some basic little hints & tips that will make life less stressful, easier & which will put on display the most important things that you are going to need access to, making your food tastier! You'll be moving with some form of elegance if everything flows well in the kitchen – no more scraping about in the back of dark drawers for forgotten implements.

KITCHEN TIPS

• So, tip number one, get an old laundry or pan rack to hang from the ceiling. These are really cheap, easy to install, look really nice & quaint, & if you want to make one look funky, just give it a lick of paint. Straight away you resolve the problem of where to put your pans, your colanders & sieves, & things like graters. It will look like cool clutter. One of the biggest problems to muck up dinner parties is lack of room to cook in & serve from, so on the day have a look at your kitchen surfaces & move all your homely family memorabilia, your old jars with coins in, funny little juicers that get used once a year, bills etc. & put them in a cupboard. You'll be surprised at how much room you've gained.

- If you can, it's always nice to have your sink near or in front of a window for good light & a bit of a view while doing the washing-up.

- For your work surface I would suggest getting a reasonably thick wooden one. You can do it economically or you can get some flashy hardwood but, most importantly, this allows you to chop straight on to the surface. Now, when my carpenter saw me doing this he nearly cried, but that's because he's never cooked a meal in his life! I think there's nothing more boring than having chopping boards all over the place. All you really need are two: one for fish & one for chicken. Anything else can be chopped straight on to your wooden surfaces & as time goes by they will look better & better. Just squirt with disinfectant after each use – it couldn't be easier! Every month or so drizzle some cheap olive oil over the wood to feed it & stop it cracking. It's always good to have your knives, bottle openers, peelers & cutlery in a drawer near your central prep area (knives can be in a block).

- Always have your larder stocked with non-perishables like oils, vinegars, spices, herbs, salts, jams, pasta, rice, mustards & tinned items. I like to keep them in those cheap recycled kilner jars that are easy to get hold of. It's good to get all sorts of different sizes & shapes. One of the cheapest shelf-saving solutions is this: every time you finish with a jar of jam or chutney, give it a wash, soak the label off & then put two screws through the lid of each jar & attach them to the bottom of a shelf. To store, just screw the jar into the lid & it will hang under the shelf – dead easy to grab. I think it looks great to have them all on display. That way you can immediately see what you've got or are running out of.

- Bins have always been an afterthought for me, & they've driven me mad for years now. The best thing is to build a bin into your kitchen work surface if you can. It's very simple: get an extra large plastic bin & either have it in a cupboard so you can pull it out, or cut a hole into your work surface so you can put all your rubbish down through it.

- If you're not going to get a ceiling unit for your pans, try using a free-standing metal or wooden shelf unit on which to stack your bowls, whisks, pans & food processors.

- The final test to find out if you've got a kitchen that's working well is to draw an aerial view showing the fridge, the spices on their shelf, the knives in their drawer or block & so on. Think of a dish that you regularly cook, then, using a red pen, draw the 'journey' of the meal, from going to the fridge, to cutting up food, to seasoning it, to getting commodities from the cupboard, & by the time you've finished & got it in the oven, if there are loads of lines crossing all over the place, you know it's not a brilliant design layout! The two main focal points are your chopping area & sink, so try to position them next to each other. As you stand at your sink, the oven should be behind you. You will become more economical in your movements & will be able to work faster.

KITCHEN EQUIPMENT

- **Pans**
  It's really important that you get yourself some sturdy pans. For home use it's best to always go with non-stick if you can – it's definitely the way forward! I work with Tefal & can say that their pans are my first choice. They're widely available, so get yourself a few from the range.

- **Cookers**
  With regard to stove-tops/hobs, I would go for gas every time – they feel more robust, more visual & seem to give you more physical control over temperature. For me, the ideal scenario would be a gas hob & an electric oven. You generally get what you pay for, but when using medium to cheaper ovens I would most definitely advise going for the larger, better-known companies, which have very good warranties, spare parts & servicing departments, as opposed to some of the design-over-content pretentious makes.

- **Knives**
  When it comes to knives, you really do get what you pay for. What I don't want you to do is go out & buy a large, cheap set, because they won't last very long. You won't go far wrong if you buy a great-quality large & small chopping knife, a paring knife & a serrated knife. Job done.

- **Dishwashers**
  I find it strange that a lot of people still don't have dishwashers even though they have space for one. They were once considered expensive, but you can get hold of them cheaply & second-hand these days. They are great for washing all your stuff – especially glassware – & because of the high temperatures they sterilize everything & are therefore more hygienic, plus they are easy to plumb in (I've always done my own).

- **Freezers & microwaves**
  There seems to be some idea that these are a bit naff, probably because prepacked frozen meals have been associated with them. The truth is that microwaves are great for reheating things for parties, wonderful for steaming, getting your butter soft, boiling things like veg quickly, & the freezer is a brilliant method of preserving food, so I think both of these are essential for the modern household.

- **Barbecues**
  My preference would be charcoal or wood barbecues, which can impart the authentic smoky flavour that makes barbecuing what it should be. Sometimes it's easy to burn things on the outside & not cook them through on the inside. But with barbecues you can organize your charcoal high on one side (hot end) & low on the other – this way you can get fast, hot, direct heat to achieve good colour & on the other side your food will cook slowly & remain tasty & juicy. I've bought myself the most amazing handmade barbecue off a bloke in Oxford. It was about two or three times the price of a really good barbecue, but it should last years because it's stainless steel & incredibly thick. You definitely get what you pay for.

Thanks...

To My darling wife Jools and my girls Poppy and DAISY for making me excited to wake up every morning...

MUM and DAD FOR READING THROUGH MY BOOK WITH A FINE-TOOTHED COMB - thanks to you both ♥

TO LORD LOFTUS ❶ WHO CONTINUES TO BE THE BEST FOOD PHOTOGRAPHER IN THE WORLD - thanks bro for pulling out the stops - and to his assistant Annabel. To CHRIS TERRY who has taken amazing reportage photos - EXCEEDINGLY enthusiastic and thanks for being supportive over the past year, and to his WIERD but LOVELY assistant DANNY! THANKS TO YOU ALL FOR the most incredible pictures.

sexy

HOWEVER I WOULD LIKE TO THANK THE FOLLOWING PEOPLE FOR WORKING SO HARD ON THE BOOK: GINNY "Cat's Bum!" ROLFE, PETE 'the gorgeous Scotsman'... BEGG, BOBBY THOMSON and EDDIE "The streaker" SEISUN. ALSO THANKS TO KELLY, TOMMY, SUE, CARLY, JENNY, BETH and NIC for his 'CARE NOTES'.

LUSCIOUS LIPS

TO MY MANAGEMENT TEAM: FROSTY the perv, Louise 'the Theydon Tongue' HOLLAND, Tessa 'The Tongue' Graham and Tara 'Leather Matrix Outfit' Donovan

Does Anyone "KNOW" WHO TANYA ROBINSON IS??? ↑ see page one 1 ?

TO JEANETTE ORREY AND HER KITCHEN STAFF AT ST PETERS PRIMARY SCHOOL IN EAST BRIDGFORD, NOTTINGHAMSHIRE. AND TO NORA SANDS AND ALL THE DINNER LADIES AT KIDBROOKE SCHOOL IN GREENWICH, LONDON.

TO MY OFFICE. TO THE ENTIRE GANG AT THE OFFICE. I LOVE YOU ALL - THANKS FOR DOING A GREAT JOB, FOR SUPPORTING ME AND PUTTING UP WITH ME!

AND A MASSIVE THANKS TO DANNY McCUBBIN, MY NEW PA, FOR SORTING OUT MY DIARY AND KEEPING MY LIFE IN ORDER - YOU KEEP ME LOOKING BEAUTIFUL BRO. WORK MORE HOURS PLEASE

I'VE HAD THE HONOUR AND PLEASURE OF WORKING WITH SOME OF THE MOST TALENTED AND DEDICATED PEOPLE IN ⬛ ON THIS PROJECT. IN NO PARTICULAR ORDER: ZOE COLLINS, ANDREW CONRAD, ROBERT THIRKELL, DOMINIQUE WALKER, LANA SALAH, GUY GILBERT, TRACEY GARRETT VANYA BARWELL. THANKS TO YOU ALL.

x chris & freddie

❍ THE TEAM WHO RUN THE CHEEKY CHOPS CHARITY FOR ME - PARTICULARLY TONY, EAMON AND SHARON. AND OF COURSE, TO ALL OF YOU WHO HAVE DONATED TO CHEEKY CHOPS, - PLEASE GIVE US SOME MORE!

AND EVEN THOUGH THIS DOESN'T REALLY HAVE ANYTHING TO DO WITH THE BOOK I'D LIKE TO THANK NICK AND LISA LYONS HENSON CORPORATE ENTERTAINMENT FOR TAKING THE STUDENTS AWAY TO WALES FOR 2 DAYS TO HELP US CHOOSE OUR FINAL FIFTEEN EVERY YEAR. I JUST WANTED TO SAY THAT I APPRECIATE IT.

IF YOU EVER NEED A WEEKEND OF TEAM BUILDING FOR YOUR COMPANY THEN PHONE THESE GUYS ON 01443 228565

TO THE PENGUIN POSSE:
TOM 'THE STREAKING SLEEPWALKER' WELDON - thanks for being the best, most supportive publisher in town. (and fairest)

JOHN 'haemorrhoid' HAMILTON for putting in 4 times more work than he's paid to do. and for loving this project as much as I do. CHRIS 'Paisley Y fronts' CALLARD, SOPHIE 'great cleavage' BREWER and the rest of the rights team, SOPHIE 'Good girl' HEWAT AND CATHERINE 'you TIGER' HAMMOND from production, ANNIE LEE AND KEITH TAYLOR FOR MAKING MY CHITTER CHATTER LEGIBLE, THE GORGEOUS TORA ORDE-POWLETT AND THE VERY HANDSOME RDB WILLIAMS IN MARKETING!

THE LOVELY KATY NICHOLSON AND SAUCY JANE OPOKO FROM PUBLICITY AND FINALLY TO ALL THE SALES TEAM FOR THEIR HARD WORK.

SOME ONE FIND THIS BIRD A MATE!

AND LAST BUT NOT LEAST, THANKS TO MY NEWLY APPOINTED, BEAUTIFUL EDITOR WHO I NICKED FROM PENGUIN - I'M THE LUCKIEST BOY IN THE WORLD! - LINDSEY JORDAN

THE GUT JORDAN

LINDSAY JORDAN (well Lindsay Evans now BUT WE STILL CALL HER JORDAN) Keep up the fake tan - next time, no white bits!

MARION⁴ DEUCHARS
THE ILLUSTRATOR
M + R + THE DOG'S

TO MY GENERAL MANAGER AT LT FIFTEEN, PAULA DUPUY, AND TO THE EXECUTIVE HEAD CHEF ARTHUR POTTS. NOT FORGETTING ALL MY STUDENTS AND THE REST OF THE GANG THERE.

DAVID GLEAVE AT LIBERTY WINES - 020 7720 5350 www.libertywines.co.uk

PATRICIA AND DAN AT LA FROMAGERIE - 020 7359 7440 www.lafromagerie.co.uk

ALL THE BOYS AT KENSINGTON PLACE FISH - 020 7243 6626

TO JEKKA THE BEST ORGANIC HERB LADY IN THE WORLD - 01454 418878 www.jekkasherbfarm.com

MAIL ORDER HERBS

GEORGE AT GOLBORNE FISHERIES 020.8960 3100

GARY AT M. MOEN & SONS - 020 7622 1624 www.moen.co.uk

HASSELBLAD AND POLAROID FOR THEIR SUPPORT AND GREAT STOCK

TO SEAN AND ALISON AT THOMAS COOK FOR A WONDERFUL EFFICIENT SERVICE

TO NIKOLAI AT THE HOLLYBUSH PUB IN HAMPSTEAD FOR HIRING OUT THE UPSTAIRS ROOM FOR THE FOOD SHOTS AT A BARGAIN PRICE.

Jamie Oliver.com

AND LAST BUT NO MEANS LEAST... THANKYOU TO EVERYONE WHO APPEARS IN PHOTOS IN THE BOOK, PARTICULARLY TO MY NAN AND TO THE LOVELY KIDS JOEL EVANS, SADIE HAMILTON, AND EVIE ROLFE FOR TAKING TIME OUT OF THEIR BUSY DAYS!

INDEX

Recipes marked v are suitable for vegetarians
Page numbers in bold indicate photography

a

almonds
v   Bakewell tart 302, **303**
v   American chop salad **110**, 111
    Andy the gasman's stew 246
apple(s)
v   quick jammy apple tart 56, **57**
v   apple pie 16, **17**
v   toffee apple tart 292, **293**
v arrabiatta sauce 40
    artichokes 172
v   gratinated artichokes 172, **173**
v   sautéed Jerusalem artichokes
        with garlic & bay leaves 172, **173**
    smashed sautéed Jerusalem artichokes
        with pancetta & sage 172, **173**
    asparagus
    stir-fried duck with sugar
        snap peas & asparagus 230, **231**
    traybaked sea bass with crispy roasted
        asparagus bundles wrapped
        in bacon 262
    aubergines
v   rigatoni with sweet tomatoes, aubergine
        & mozzarella 194–5, **195**
    avocados
    Parmesan fish fillets with avocado &
        cress salad 66, **66**
v awesome spinach & ricotta
        cannelloni 198–200, **199, 201**

b

bacon
    farfalle with carbonara &
        spring peas **196**, 197
    good old liver & bacon with
        a twist **228**, 229
    traybaked sea bass with
        crispy roasted asparagus bundles
        wrapped in bacon 262
v baked pears with wine &
        scrumptious walnut cream 286, **287**
v Bakewell tart 302, **303**
v banana & blueberry French toast 98, **99**
    basil
    the best lamb cutlets with special
        basil sauce 218, **219**
    the best prawn sandwich with basil
        mayonnaise & cress 84, 85
v   cream 306, **307**
    pesto see under pesto
    squashed fig, basil & Parma ham
        sarnie in tomato bread 82, **83**
v   sweet potato topped with chillies,
        buffalo mozzarella & pesto 13

    tomato sauce with fish,
        olives & pesto 44, **45**
    bay leaves
v   sautéed Jerusalem artichokes with garlic
        & bay leaves 172, **173**
    beans
v   good old French bean salad **136**, 137
v   Moroccan-style broad bean salad with
        yoghurt & crunchy bits 108, **109**
    pan-cooked giant prawns with mangetout,
        peas & butter beans 268, **269**
    slow-roasted spiced pork loin with black-
        eyed beans & tomatoes **244**, 245
    traybaked chicken Maryland **220**, 221
    beef
    Andy the gasman's stew 246
    the best roast beef sandwich with
        crunchy lettuce, English mustard
        & gherkins 87, **87**
    Japanese-style Saturday
        night steak 130, **131**
    Jools's favourite beef stew 238, **239**
    with pak choi, mushrooms & noodles 69, **69**
    paprika sirloin steak wrap 70, **70**
    Scottish Pete's cheesy steak sandwich **94**, 95
    simple baked lasagne 8, 9, **10–11**
    the ultimate burger & chips 6–7, **7**
    beetroot
v   mini jackets topped with beetroot,
        cottage cheese & horseradish 13
v   raw beetroot salad 120, **121**
    the best chicken & sweet leek pie
        with flaky pastry 24, **25**
    the best lamb cutlets with special
        basil sauce 218, **219**
    the best prawn sandwich with
        basil mayonnaise & cress **84**, 85
    the best roast beef sandwich with
        crunchy lettuce, English mustard
        & gherkins 87, **87**
    the best roasted turnips 162, **163**
    the best sausage & super mash
        with onion gravy 4, **5**
    black-eyed beans
    slow-roasted spiced pork loin with black-eyed
        beans & tomatoes **244**, 245
    blueberries
v   banana & blueberry French toast 98, **99**
v boiled turnips with thyme
        beurre blanc 162, **163**
v braised spinach 170
    Breville 90–91
    broad beans
v   Moroccan-style broad bean salad with
        yoghurt & crunchy bits 108, **109**
    broth, feel-good chicken 156, **157**
v bruschetta with pesto 36, **37**
    the ultimate burger & chips 6–7, **7**
    butter beans
    pan-cooked giant prawns with mangetout,
        peas & butter beans 268, **269**

c

v cannelloni, awesome spinach
      & ricotta 198–200, **199, 201**
   carrot(s) 164
v   carrots boiled with orange, garlic
         & herbs 164, **165**
v   carrot & coriander crunch salad 134, **135**
v   mashed carrots 164, **164**
v   roasted carrots with orange,
         garlic & thyme 164, **165**
v cheat's dessert **298**, 299
   Cheddar
v   double-decker Cheddar cheese sandwich
         with pickled onions & crisps 88, **89**
   cheese
v   awesome spinach & ricotta
         cannelloni 198–200, **199, 201**
v   ciabatta sandwich of grilled vegetables
         with pesto & mozzarella 80, **81**
v   double-decker Cheddar cheese sandwich
         with pickled onions & crisps 88, **89**
      mini calzones with prosciutto, mozzarella
         & tomato 56, **57**
      Parmesan fish fillets with
         avocado & cress salad 66, **66**
v   Parmesan twists 54, **57**
v   pasta with sweet tomato
         sauce & baked ricotta **186**, 187
v   pesto with mozzarella 38, **39**
v   quesadillas with guacamole **100**, 101
v   quick tomato macaroni cheese 204, **205**
v   rigatoni with sweet tomatoes,
         aubergine & mozzarella 194–5, **195**
      Scottish Pete's cheesy steak sandwich **94**, 95
v   tagliatelle with spinach,
         mascarpone & Parmesan 188, **189**
v   three cheeses with chives
         filling for jacket potatoes 12
v   tomato sauce with Portabello
         mushrooms & taleggio 44, **45**
v   tomato sauce with tagliatelle, spinach
         & goat's cheese 42, **42**
   chicken
      the best chicken & sweet leek pie
         with flaky pastry 24, **25**
      chicken tikka masala **28**, 29
      everyday crispy chicken with
         sweet tomatoes 222, **223**
      feel-good chicken broth 156, **157**
      gingered chicken with noodles 68, **68**
      pesto with roasted chicken 36, **37**
      roast chicken with lemon &
         rosemary roast potatoes 18, **19**
      spring poached chicken 232, **233**
      super-tasty Spanish roast chicken 216, **217**
      traybaked chicken Maryland 220, **221**
   chickpeas
      lamb with chickpeas, yoghurt
         & roasted veg 242, **243**
      scrumptious Spanish chickpea &
         chorizo soup 144, **145**

v   summer chickpea salad 122, 123
   chillies
v   arrabiatta sauce 40
      laksa-style scallops with
         sweet chilli sauce 252, **253**
v   stir-fried corn with chilli,
         ginger, garlic & parsley **166**, 167
v   sweet potato topped with
         chillies, buffalo mozzarella & basil 13
v chips 6, **7**, 21, **22**
   chives
v   three cheeses with chives filling for
         jacket potatoes 12
   chocolate
v   chocolate clafoutis with caramelized
         oranges 294, **295**
v   sweet vanilla risotto with poached
         peaches & chocolate 288, **289**
   chorizo
      chorizo & tomato omelette 67, **67**
      scrumptious Spanish chickpea &
         chorizo soup 144, **145**
v ciabatta sandwich of grilled vegetables
      with pesto & mozzarella 80, **81**
   coconut
v   crunchy Keralan salad 112, **113**
   concertina squid 276, **277**
v cool crudité veggies with a
      minted pea & yoghurt dip 128, **129**
   coriander
v   carrot & coriander crunch salad 134, **135**
   cottage cheese
v   mini jackets topped with beetroot, cottage
         cheese & horseradish 13
   couscous
      with super-tasty lamb cutlets 71, **71**
      omega 3 & couscous 270, **271**
      salmon & couscous 64, **64**
   crab, crème fraîche, spring onions, chilli &
      mint filling for jacket potatoes 12
v creamed corn 167, **167**
v creams, scented English 306, **307**
   crème fraîche
      crab, crème fraîche, spring
         onions, chilli & mint filling for
         jacket potatoes 12
      smoked salmon, lemon &
         crème fraîche sandwich 92, **93**
   cress
      the best prawn sandwich with basil
         mayonnaise & cress 84, **85**
v   crunchy Keralan salad 112, **113**
      Parmesan fish fillets with
         avocado & cress salad 66, **66**
   crispy Peking duck in pancakes 102
v crumble, stewed fruit 52, **53**
v crunchy Keralan salad 112, **113**
   curry
      chicken tikka masala **28**, 29
v   curried spinach 170

d

desserts
- v apple pie 16, **17**
- v baked pears with wine &
  scrumptious walnut cream 286, **287**
- v Bakewell tart 302, **303**
- v banana & blueberry French toast 98, **99**
- v cheat's 298, **299**
- v chocolate clafoutis with
  caramelized oranges 294, **295**
- v maple syrup & pecan tart 300, **301**
- v quick jammy apple tart 56, **57**
- v scented English creams 306, **307**
- v stewed fruit crumble 52, **53**
- v stewed fruit syllabub 52, **53**
- v stewed fruit on toast 52, **53**
- v sticky toffee pudding 304, **305**
- v sweet vanilla risotto with
  poached peaches & chocolate 288, **289**
- v toffee apple tart 292, **293**
- v the ultimate jam roly poly 296
- v **dip, minted pea & yoghurt 128**, 129
- v **double-decker Cheddar cheese sandwich
  with pickled onions & crisps 88, 89**

duck
- crispy Peking duck in pancakes 102
- stir-fried duck with sugar
  snap peas & asparagus 230, **231**
- sweet duck legs cooked with
  plums & star anise 236, **237**

dumplings
- slow-cooked lamb with my mum's dumplings 48

e

**everyday crispy chicken
with sweet tomatoes 222, 223**

f

the famous jacket potato 12–13, 14–15
- crab, crème fraîche, spring
  onions, chilli & mint filling 12
- v mini jackets topped with beetroot,
  cottage cheese & horseradish 13
- prawns & Marie Rose sauce filling 12
- smoked salmon & soured cream filling 13
- v sweet potato topped with
  chillies, buffalo mozzarella & basil 13
- v three cheeses with chives filling 12

**farfalle with carbonara &
spring peas 196, 197**
feel-good chicken broth 156, 157

figs
- squashed fig, basil & Parma ham sarnie
  in tomato bread 82, **83**
- v **filo pastry parcels with stewed fruit 52**

fish
- fish & chips & mushy peas 21, **22–3**
- grilled & traybaked
  ratatouille with white fish 260, **261**
- Italian-style upside-down fish pie 256, **257**
- the nicest traybaked lemon sole 274, **275**
- Parmesan fish fillets with
  avocado & cress salad 66, **66**
- with pesto 36, **37**
- southern Indian rice &
  seafood soup 152, **153**
- spiced fried fish with a
  speedy tartare sauce **258**, 259
- tasty fish bake 264, **265**
- tomato sauce with fish,
  olives & basil 44, **45**
- *see also* individual names

fishcakes, South American 280
French beans
- v good old French bean salad **136**, 137

French-style peas 179
fruit, stewed *see* stewed fruit

g

garlic
- v carrots boiled with orange,
  garlic & herbs 164, **165**
- v pasta bianca 184, **185**
- v roasted carrots with orange,
  garlic & thyme 164, **165**
- v sautéed Jerusalem artichokes
  with garlic & bay leaves 172, **173**
- v stir-fried corn with chilli,
  ginger, garlic & parsley **166**, 167

ginger
- gingered chicken with noodles 68, **68**
- v stir-fried corn with chilli,
  ginger, garlic & parsley **166**, 167

ginger biscuits
- v cheat's dessert **298**, 299

goat's cheese
- v tomato sauce with tagliatelle, spinach
  & goat's cheese 42, **42**
- v **good old French bean salad 136**, 137
good old liver & bacon with a twist 228, 229
- v **gratinated artichokes 172, 173**
gravy, onion 4
**grilled & traybaked ratatouille
with white fish 260, 261**
- v **guacamole, quesadillas with 100**, 101

h

haddock
- South American fishcakes 280
ham, roasted marmalade 226, 227
herbs
- v carrots boiled with orange,
  garlic & herbs 164, **165**

horseradish
- v mini jackets topped with beetroot,
  cottage cheese & horseradish 13
- smoked trout, horseradish
  & new potato salad 118, **119**
- v summer tomato &
  horseradish salad **116**, 117

hot tuna salad 65, 65

i

Italian-style upside-down fish pie 256, **257**

j

jacket potatoes *see* the famous jacket potato
Japanese-style Saturday
   night steak 130, **131**
Jerusalem artichokes *see* artichokes
Jools's favourite beef stew 238, **239**

k

v kebabs, vegetable, with pesto 38, **39**
   kitchen equipment 310–11
   kitchen tips 308–10
   kitchens 308

l

laksa-style scallops with
   sweet chilli sauce 252, **253**
lamb
   with chickpeas, yoghurt
      & roasted veg 242, **243**
   best lamb cutlets with special
      basil sauce 218, **219**
   super-tasty lamb cutlets 71, **71**
lamb, slow-cooked
   with my mum's dumplings 48
   ragù pasta 48, **49**
   shepherd's pie 48, **49**
   shoulder of lamb with
      roasted vegetables 46, **47**
lasagne, simple baked **8**, 9, **10–11**
leeks
   the best chicken & sweet leek pie
      with flaky pastry 24, **25**
lemon sole, traybaked 274, **275**
liver
   good old liver & bacon
      with a twist **228**, 229
lunchbox 76–8

m

macaroni
v quick tomato macaroni cheese 204, **205**
mangetout
   pan-cooked giant prawns with mangetout,
      peas & butter beans 268, **269**
v maple syrup & pecan tart 300, **301**
v marinated peppers 174, **175**
marmalade
   roasted marmalade ham 226, **227**
mascarpone
v tagliatelle with spinach, mascarpone
      & Parmesan 188, **189**
v mashed carrots 164, **164**

mini calzones with prosciutto,
   mozzarella & tomato 56, **57**
v mini jackets topped with beetroot, cottage
      cheese & horseradish 13
mint
v cool crudité veggies with a minted pea
      & yoghurt dip **128**, 129
v Moroccan-style broad bean salad
      with yoghurt & crunchy bits 108, **109**
mozzarella
v ciabatta sandwich of grilled vegetables
      with pesto & mozzarella 80, **81**
   mini calzones with prosciutto,
      mozzarella & tomato 56, **57**
v pesto with mozzarella 38, **39**
v rigatoni with sweet tomatoes,
      aubergine & mozzarella 194–5, **195**
v sweet potato topped with
      chillies, buffalo mozzarella & basil 13
mushrooms
   beef with pak choi, mushrooms
      & noodles 69, **69**
   lamb cutlets with special
      basil sauce 218, **219**
v the real mushroom soup **148**, 149
v tomato sauce with Portabello mushrooms
      & taleggio 44, **45**
mussels with pesto 36, **37**

n

the nicest traybaked lemon sole 274, **275**
noodles
   beef with pak choi, mushrooms
      & noodles 69, **69**
   gingered chicken with noodles 68, **68**

o

olives
v spaghetti with uncooked tomato,
      rocket & olive sauce **192**, 193
   tomato sauce with fish,
      olives & basil 44, **45**
omega 3 & couscous 270, **271**
omelette, chorizo & tomato 67, **67**
onion(s)
   the best sausage & super mash
      with onion gravy 4, **5**
v sweet red onion pasta 210
v the ultimate onion soup 146, **147**
orange(s)
v & cardamom cream 306, **307**
v carrots boiled with orange,
      garlic & herbs 164, **165**
v cheat's dessert **298**, 299
v chocolate clafoutis with
      caramelized oranges 294, **295**
v roasted carrots with orange,
      garlic & thyme 164, **165**

p

pak choi
beef with pak choi, mushrooms
& noodles 69, **69**

pancakes
crispy Peking duck in pancakes 102

pancetta
farfalle with carbonara & spring peas **196**, 197
smashed sautéed Jerusalem artichokes with
pancetta & sage 172, **173**

**pan-cooked giant prawns with mangetout,
peas & butter beans** 268, **269**

paprika sirloin steak wrap 70, **70**

Parma ham
squashed fig, basil & Parma ham sarnie
in tomato bread 82, **83**

Parmesan
Parmesan fish fillets with avocado
& cress salad 66, **66**
v tagliatelle with spinach,
mascarpone & Parmesan 188, **189**
v Parmesan twists 54, **57**

parsley
v stir-fried corn with chilli, ginger,
garlic & parsley **166**, 167

pasta
v awesome spinach & ricotta
cannelloni 198–200, **199**, **201**
farfalle with carbonara &
spring peas **196**, 197
v pasta bianca 184, **185**
v pasta peperonata 208, **209**
v pasta with sweet tomato sauce &
baked ricotta 186, 187
v quick tomato macaroni cheese 204, **205**
ragù pasta 48, **49**
v rigatoni with sweet tomatoes,
aubergine & mozzarella 194–5, **195**
simple baked lasagne 8, 9, **10–11**
v spaghetti with uncooked tomato,
rocket & olive sauce **192**, 193
v sweet red onion pasta 210
v tagliatelle with spinach,
mascarpone & Parmesan 188, **189**
v tomato sauce with tagliatelle,
spinach & goat's cheese 42, **42**
v tomato sauces for pasta 40
working girl's pasta **206**, 207

v **peaches**
sweet vanilla risotto with poached
peaches & chocolate **288**, 289

v **pears**
baked pears with wine &
scrumptious walnut cream 286, **287**

peas 179
v cool crudité veggies with a
minted pea & yoghurt dip **128**, 129
v easy peas 179
farfalle with carbonara &
spring peas **196**, 197
fish, chips & mushy peas 21, **22–3**
French-style peas 179
pan-cooked giant prawns with mangetout,
peas & butter beans 268, **269**

v **pecans**
maple syrup & pecan tart 300, **301**

v **peppers** 174
v marinated 174, **175**
v pasta peperonata 208, **209**
v Spanish-style peppered potatoes 174

v **pesto** 34, **35**
v with bruschetta 36, **37**
v ciabatta sandwich of grilled vegetables
with pesto & mozzarella 80, **81**
with fish 36, **37**
v with mixed tomato salad 38, **39**
v with mozzarella 38, **39**
with mussels 36, **37**
with roasted chicken 36, **37**
v with roasted vegetables 38, **39**
v with vegetable kebabs 38, **39**

pies
v apple pie 16, **17**
the best chicken & sweet leek pie
with flaky pastry 24, **25**

plums
sweet duck legs cooked with plums
& star anise **236**, 237

polenta
Italian-style upside-down fish pie 256, **257**
tomato sauce with grilled polenta 43, **43**

pork
simple baked lasagne 8, 9, **10–11**
slow-roasted spiced pork loin with black-
eyed beans & tomatoes **244**, 245

potatoes
the best sausage & super mash
with onion gravy 4, **5**
concertina squid 276, **277**
the famous jacket potato 12–13, **14–15**
fish & chips & mushy peas 21
roast chicken with lemon &
rosemary roast potatoes 18, **19**
smoked trout, horseradish
& new potato salad 118, **119**
v Spanish-style peppered potatoes 174
tasty fish bake 264, **265**
the ultimate burger & chips 6–7, **7**

prawn(s)
the best prawn sandwich with
basil mayonnaise & cress **84**, 85
laksa-style scallops with
sweet chilli sauce 252, **253**
& Marie Rose sauce filling
for jacket potatoes 12
pan-cooked giant prawns with mangetout,
peas & butter beans 268, **269**
tomato sauce with marinated
jumbo prawns 44, **45**

prosciutto
  mini calzones with prosciutto,
    mozzarella & tomato 56, **57**
  with turnips 162
puff pastry 54
v quick jammy apple tart 56, **57**
  mini calzones with prosciutto,
    mozzarella & tomato 56, **57**
v Parmesan twists 54, **57**
  sausage rolls 56, **57**
v pumpkin rice laksa soup 142–3, **143**
  puttanesca sauce 40

q

v quesadillas with guacamole **100**, 101
v quick jammy apple tart 56, **57**
v quick tomato macaroni cheese 204, **205**

r

ragù pasta 48, **49**
ratatouille
  grilled & traybaked ratatouille
    with white fish 260, **261**
v raw beetroot salad 120, **121**
v the real mushroom soup **148**, 149
red mullet
  omega 3 & couscous 270, **271**
rice
v pumpkin rice laksa soup 142–3, **143**
  southern Indian rice &
    seafood soup **152**, 153
v sweet vanilla risotto with poached
    peaches & chocolate **288**, 289
ricotta
v awesome spinach & ricotta
    cannelloni 198–200, **199**, **201**
v pasta with sweet tomato
    sauce & baked ricotta **186**, 187
v rigatoni with sweet tomatoes,
    aubergine & mozzarella 194–5, **195**
risotto
v sweet vanilla risotto with poached
    peaches & chocolate **288,** 289
roast chicken, super-tasty Spanish 216, **217**
roast chicken with lemon &
    rosemary roast potatoes 18, **19**
v roasted carrots with orange,
    garlic & thyme 164, **165**
roasted chicken with pesto 36, **37**
roasted marmalade ham 226, **227**
roasted turnips 162, **163**
v roasted vegetables with pesto 38, **39**
rocket
v spaghetti with uncooked tomato,
    rocket & olive sauce **192**, 193
rosemary
  roast chicken with lemon &
    rosemary roast potatoes 18, **19**

s

sage
  smashed sautéed Jerusalem artichokes
    with pancetta & sage 172, **173**
salads
v American chop salad **110**, 111
v carrot & coriander crunch salad 134, **135**
v cool crudité veggies with a
    minted pea & yoghurt dip **128**, 129
v crunchy Keralan salad 112, **113**
v good old French bean salad **136**, 137
  hot tuna salad 65, **65**
  Japanese-style Saturday
    night steak 130, **131**
v Moroccan-style broad bean salad
    with yoghurt & crunchy bits 108, **109**
  Parmesan fish fillets with
    avocado & cress 66, **66**
v pesto with mixed tomato salad 38, **39**
v raw beetroot salad 120, **121**
  smoked trout, horseradish
    & new potato salad 118, **119**
v summer chickpea salad 122, **123**
v summer tomato &
    horseradish salad **116**, 117
v Thai watermelon salad 126, **127**
salmon
  & couscous 64, **64**
  summer traybaked salmon **254**, 255
  see also smoked salmon
sandwiches
v banana & blueberry French toast 98, **99**
  the best prawn sandwich with
    basil mayonnaise & cress **84**, 85
  the best roast beef sandwich with
    crunchy lettuce, English mustard
    & gherkins 87, **87**
  Breville toasted sandwiches 90–91
v ciabatta sandwich of grilled vegetables
    with pesto & mozzarella 80, **81**
  crispy Peking duck in pancakes 102
v double-decker Cheddar cheese sandwich with
    pickled onions & crisps 88, **89**
v quesadillas with guacamole **100**, 101
  Scottish Pete's cheesy steak sandwich **94**, 95
  smoked salmon, lemon &
    crème fraîche sandwich 92, **93**
  squashed fig, basil & Parma ham
    sarnie in tomato bread 82, **83**
sardines
  omega 3 & couscous 270, **271**
sauces
v arrabiatta 40
  puttanesca 40
v simple tomato sauce 40
v tartare sauce **258**, 259
sausage rolls 56, **57**
sausages
  the best sausage & super mash
    with onion gravy 4, **5**

tomato sauce with sausages 44, **45**

v   sautéed Jerusalem artichokes
          with garlic & bay leaves 172, **173**
    scallops
          laksa-style scallops with
              sweet chilli sauce 252, **253**
v   scented English creams 306, **307**
    Scottish Pete's cheesy steak sandwich 94, **95**
    scrumptious Spanish chickpea &
          chorizo soup 144, **145**
    sea bass
          traybaked sea bass with crispy roasted
              asparagus bundles wrapped in bacon 262
    seafood
          southern Indian rice & seafood soup **152**, 153
    shepherd's pie 48, **49**
    simple tomato sauce 40
    skate simmered in a sweet
          tomato sauce 266–7
    slow-cooked shoulder of lamb
          with roasted vegetables 46, **47**
    slow-roasted spiced pork loin with black-
          eyed beans & tomatoes **244**, 245
    smashed sautéed Jerusalem artichokes
          with pancetta & sage 172, **173**
    smoked salmon
          smoked salmon, lemon &
              crème fraîche sandwich 92, **93**
          smoked salmon & soured cream filling
              for jacket potatoes 13
    smoked trout, horseradish &
          new potato salad 118, **119**
    sole
          the nicest traybaked lemon sole 274, **275**
    soups
          feel-good chicken broth 156, **157**
v   pumpkin rice laksa 142–3, **143**
v   the real mushroom soup **148**, 149
          scrumptious Spanish chickpea &
              chorizo soup 144, **145**
          southern Indian rice & seafood soup **152**, 153
v   tomato soup 26, **27**
v   the ultimate onion soup 146, **147**
    South American fishcakes 280
    southern Indian rice &
          seafood soup **152**, 153
v   spaghetti with uncooked tomato,
          rocket & olive sauce **192**, 193
v   Spanish-style peppered potatoes 174
    spiced fried fish with a
          speedy tartare sauce **258**, 259
    spinach 170
v   awesome spinach & ricotta
              cannelloni 198–200, **199**, **201**
v   curried spinach 170
v   perfect braised spinach 170
v   tagliatelle with spinach,
              mascarpone & Parmesan 188, **189**
v   tomato sauce with tagliatelle,
              spinach & goat's cheese 42, **42**

v   wonderful creamed spinach 170
    spring poached chicken 232, **233**
    squashed fig, basil & Parma ham
          sarnie in tomato bread 82, **83**
    squid, concertina 276, **277**
    star anise
v   strawberry & star anise cream 306, **307**
          sweet duck legs cooked with
              plums & star anise **236**, 237
v   stewed fruit **50**, 51
v   crumble 52, **53**
v   filo pastry parcels 52
v   syllabub 52, **53**
v   on toast 52, **53**
v   with yoghurt 52
    stews
          Andy the gasman's stew 246
          Jools's favourite beef stew 238, **239**
v   sticky toffee pudding 304, 305
v   stir-fried corn with chilli,
          ginger, garlic & parsley **166**, 167
    stir-fried duck with sugar
          snap peas & asparagus 230, **231**
v   strawberry & star anise cream 306, **307**
    sugar snap peas
          stir-fried duck with sugar snap peas
              & asparagus 230, **231**
v   summer chickpea salad 122, **123**
v   summer tomato &
          horseradish salad **116**, 117
    summer traybaked salmon **254**, 255
    super-tasty lamb cutlets 71, **71**
    super-tasty Spanish roast chicken 216, **217**
    sweet duck legs cooked with
          plums & star anise **236**, 237
v   sweet potato topped with chillies,
          buffalo mozzarella & basil 13
v   sweet red onion pasta 210
v   sweet vanilla risotto with poached
          peaches & chocolate **288**, 289
    sweetcorn 166
v   with butter, salt & pepper 166
v   creamed 167, **167**
v   stir-fried corn with chilli,
              ginger, garlic & parsley **166**, 167
          traybaked chicken Maryland **220**, 221
v   syllabub, stewed fruit 52, **53**

t

    tagliatelle
v   pasta bianca 184, **185**
v   with spinach, mascarpone
              & Parmesan 188, **189**
v   tomato sauce with tagliatelle,
              spinach & goat's cheese 42, **42**
    taleggio
v   tomato sauce with Portabello mushrooms
              & taleggio 44, **45**
v   tartare sauce **258**, 259

tarts
v   Bakewell tart 303, **303**
v   quick jammy apple tart 56, **57**
v   maple syrup & pecan tart 300, **301**
v   toffee apple tart 292, **293**
v   **Thai watermelon salad** 126, **127**
thyme
v   boiled turnips with thyme
        beurre blanc 162, **163**
v   roasted carrots with orange,
        garlic & thyme 164, **165**
v   **toast, stewed fruit on** 52
toasted sandwiches 90–91
v   **toffee apple tart** 292, **293**
v   **toffee pudding, sticky 304**, 305
v   **tomato sauce, simple** 40
        with fish, olives & basil 44, **45**
v   with grilled polenta 42, **43**
        with marinated jumbo prawns 44, **45**
v   for pasta 40
v   with Portabello mushrooms
        & taleggio 44, **45**
        with sausages 44, **45**
v   with tagliatelle, spinach
        & goat's cheese 42, **42**
tomato(es)
    chorizo & tomato omelette 67, **67**
    everyday crispy chicken with
        sweet tomatoes 222, **223**
    mini calzones with prosciutto,
        mozzarella & 56, **57**
v   pasta with sweet tomato
        sauce & baked ricotta **186**, 187
v   pesto with mixed tomato
        salad 38, **39**
v   quick tomato macaroni cheese 204, **205**
v   rigatoni with sweet tomatoes,
        aubergine & mozzarella 194–5, **195**
v   simple tomato sauce 40
    skate simmered in a sweet
        tomato sauce 266–7
    slow-roasted spiced pork loin with
        black-eyed beans & 244, **245**
v   soup 26, **27**
v   spaghetti with uncooked tomato,
        rocket & olive sauce **192**, 193
v   summer tomato & horseradish salad **116**, 117
tasty fish bake 264, **265**
**tender & crisp chicken
        legs with sweet tomatoes** 222, **223**
tortillas
    paprika sirloin steak wrap 70, **70**
traybaked chicken Maryland 220, 221
v   **traybaked lemon sole** 274, **275**
**traybaked sea bass with crispy roasted
        asparagus bundles wrapped in bacon**
        262
trout
    tasty fish bake 264, **265**

tuna
    hot tuna salad 65, **65**
    working girl's pasta **206**, 207
turnips 162
v   boiled turnips with thyme
        beurre blanc 162, **163**
    turnips with prosciutto 162
    the best roasted turnips 162, **163**

u

the ultimate burger & chips 6–7, **7**
v   **the ultimate jam roly poly** 296
v   **the ultimate onion soup** 146, **147**

v

vanilla
v   sweet vanilla risotto with poached
        peaches & chocolate **288**, 289
vegetables
v   ciabatta sandwich of grilled vegetables
        with pesto & mozzarella 80, **81**
v   cool crudité veggies with a
        minted pea & yoghurt dip 128, **129**
    grilled & traybaked
        ratatouille with white fish 260, **261**
    lamb with chickpeas, yoghurt
        & roasted vegetables 242, **243**
v   pesto with roasted vegetables 38, **39**
v   pesto with vegetable kebabs **38,** 39
    slow-cooked shoulder of lamb
        with roasted vegetables 46, **47**
    see also individual names

w

walnuts
v   baked pears with wine & scrumptious
        walnut cream 286, **287**
watermelon
v   Thai watermelon salad 126, **127**
wine
v   baked pears with wine & scrumptious
        walnut cream 286, **287**
v   wonderful creamed spinach 170
    working girl's pasta **206**, 207

y

yoghurt
v   cool crudité veggies with a
        minted pea & yoghurt dip **128**, 129
    lamb with chickpeas, yoghurt
        & roasted veg 242, **243**
v   Moroccan-style broad bean salad
        with yoghurt & crunchy bits 108, **109**
v   stewed fruit with yoghurt 52